Praise for *My Seven Black Fathers*

"Research tells us that Black boys who have access to Black fathers and mentors in their communities have a much better chance of navigating the world successfully and overcoming systemic racism to achieve their full potential. Will Jawando's story poignantly demonstrates this point but also provides critical insight into the form and structure of these relationships, and the power they have not only to transform the lives of Black boys but to rebuild whole communities."
—Arne Duncan, former U.S. Secretary of Education

"With dignity, clarity, and compassion, Will Jawando takes readers on a tour of his past through the stories of seven men who mentored, protected, and loved him along the road to adulthood. Written in a voice that is simultaneously bright, sanguine, and affecting, *My Seven Black Fathers* is an inspiring personal narrative, but it is not an ordinary memoir. Instead, the book is a guidebook on the essential gift of mentorship and how staggeringly transformative it was in the life of one beautiful Black boy. But most of all, *My Seven Black Fathers* is a praise song to the mysteries of human connection and the resilience that is an inherent part of African American identity."
—Emily Bernard, author of *Black Is the Body*

"A passionate 'love letter to Black men' . . . Candid and uplifting . . . This book is a clarion call to families and communities to provide crucial support to young people, particularly young Black men."
—Andrienne Cruz, *Booklist* (starred review)

T000007S

WILL JAWANDO

MY SEVEN BLACK FATHERS

Will Jawando is an attorney, an activist, a community leader, and a councilmember in Montgomery County, Maryland, a diverse community of more than one million residents. Called "the progressive leader we need" by the late congressman John Lewis, Jawando has worked with Speaker Nancy Pelosi, Senator Sherrod Brown, and President Barack Obama. His writing has appeared in *The Washington Post* and *The Root* and on BET.com, and his work has been featured in *The New York Times* and *New York* magazine and on NPR, NBC News, and MTV. He regularly appears on CNN, MSNBC, and other media outlets.

MY SEVEN BLACK FATHERS

◆◆◆◆◆◆◆

A Memoir of Race, Family,

and the Mentors Who Made Me Whole

WILL JAWANDO

PICADOR
Farrar, Straus and Giroux
New York

To my beloved children, Alia, Addison, Ava, and William Isaiah,
I pray I learned these lessons of fatherhood well

◆ ◆ ◆

Picador
120 Broadway, New York 10271

The Library of Congress has cataloged the Farrar, Straus and Giroux
hardcover edition as follows:
Names: Jawando, Will, 1983– author.
Title: My seven Black fathers : a young activist's memoir of race, family,
    and the mentors who made him whole / Will Jawando.
Description: First edition. | New York : Farrar, Straus and Giroux, 2022.
Identifiers: LCCN 2021057147 | ISBN 9780374604875 (hardcover)
Subjects: LCSH: Jawando, Will, 1983– —Childhood and youth. | African
    American men—Maryland—Montgomery County—Biography. |
    African Americans—Maryland—Social conditions. | African Americans—
    Maryland—Biography. | Role models—Maryland—Biography. | Nigerian
    Americans—Maryland—Biography. | Montgomery County (Md.)—Biography.
Classification: LCC F187.M7 J39 2022 | DDC 9752/8400496073—
    dc23/eng/20211221
LC record available at https://lccn.loc.gov/2021057147

Paperback ISBN: 978-1-250-86718-6

Designed by Janet Evans-Scanlon

10 9 8 7 6 5 4 3 2 1

CONTENTS

MY SEVEN
BLACK FATHERS

INTRODUCTION

KALFANI AND I MET ON THE SCHOOL BASKETBALL COURT IN fifth grade. It was the late eighties, early nineties, the "golden age of basketball," a time when Black players dominated the sport *and* pop culture. Kareem Abdul-Jabbar's skyhook, executed with unprecedented coordination and precision, would help him become the NBA's all-time leading scorer. Hakeem Olajuwon's dream shake made him almost impossible to defend against. Shaq, the all-star center and the face of Toys for Tots, starred in his own video game. And then there was the iconic image called "Jumpman" of Michael Jordan soaring through the air from the free throw line, one arm outstretched toward the hoop, the other palm spread at his side as if to squelch gravity. More than a logo, "Jumpman" remains a symbol of potential, excellence, and the dream of being not only the best but also the greatest.

A segregated institution until the 1950s, the NBA cultivated the status of Black men as global role models and icons for *all* Americans. But for Black boys, Black athletes have always felt like they belonged to us. Once, our heroes practiced jump shots in dusty schoolyards just like we did. This fact meant the possibility existed for us to play in front of millions of fans, just like them, if we gave it everything we had.

The confidence that the famous ballers exuded I craved from the time I was in fifth grade. Above all, I sought a sense of belonging. For a biracial Black boy raised by a white mother who had split from my Nigerian father, basketball became my entry point to an authentic Black identity. In my neighborhood of Long Branch, a mostly Black, brown, and immigrant working-class community in Silver Spring, Maryland, right outside DC, basketball defined Black boyhood. You proved yourself on the asphalt court, and at my school, the gatekeeper of that court was Kalfani.

As a nine-year-old, I remember first peering at Kalfani playing through a chain-link fence. Brown-skinned, keen-featured, and long-limbed, Kalfani was a natural-born leader. For weeks I watched from afar as each boy made his way to the three-point line and had his shot at becoming "captain." Kalfani was usually the first to make a basket, with a perfectly formed jump shot that flew high in the air and more often than not hit the net only. Kalfani judiciously picked the teams, matching each player with a worthy competitor. He also called all the fouls and outs, and the other boys, across grade levels, looked to him for guidance.

Watching my classmates gathered on the court to serve up braggadocios, dreams, and layups, I thought their goals of besting Reggie Miller's three-point percentage or getting drafted to the NBA seemed totally reachable. In my eyes, they were capable of magic, while I, incapable of handling rejection, never dared ask if I could play. Then, one day, Kalfani shouted, "We short a man!" With only nine players, the five-on-five game would become four-on-four and one boy would have to sit out. The boys were already arguing who would take the bench.

"Hey, you!" Kalfani waved in my direction. "You wanna play?"

I glanced around. He was talking to *me*, the quintessential onlooker. After taking a deep breath, I jogged to the court, little bursts of nausea rising with each footfall. I even stumbled, but the boys were too busy getting hyped up for the game to notice. This was a little like being invited to dance when you have no idea where to place your feet. But things began to roll. The opposing offense loosened his shoulders, called "Check!" and threw to his defender. The defender passed back; the game began. Almost immediately I was winded and struggled to keep up. But after a few minutes something in my body clicked *on* while something in my mind clicked *off*. I stopped thinking about how I played and started to play.

Kalfani launched a chest pass to me, and I staggered backward a bit, but somehow I managed to hang on to the ball. While the other boys chuckled, Kalfani flashed over to the hoop with his right arm raised high in the air, screaming, "I'm open! I'm open!" Breathless but wired, I passed him the ball, he drove in for a layup, and just like that, I had my first ever assist.

After that day, Kalfani took me under his wing. It never occurred to me back then to ask him, "Why me?" and unfortunately, I would never get that chance. We would meet up before the other boys got to the court and take turns shooting or rebounding for each other. He made shooting the ball from the three-point line look effortless. I would put everything into trying to get the ball in the net, throwing it up with both hands, only for the ball to ricochet off the basket, rattling the entire post.

"Just keep shooting," he'd say before passing me the ball again. And again. And again. "You just gotta practice."

Kalfani and I didn't only play ball together. We met at the corner of Wayne Avenue and Fenton Street in downtown Silver Spring to walk to school together in the mornings. Kalfani would often walk with me the few blocks to my parents' office when school let out, and we hung out at each other's homes on the weekends.

Kalfani's building reminded me of where I lived with my mother after my parents divorced. The lock on the lobby door was busted. The scent of urine hung in the vestibule where supermarket circulars were scattered on the floor. A fluorescent light bulb flickered and buzzed in the permanently out-of-service elevator. Sometimes there were older boys on the stairs smoking weed and talking smack. Kalfani nodded at them, gave and received pounds. No one extended their hand to me, and I didn't test the waters by offering my own. These boys had known one another all their lives. I had known Kalfani for only a few months back then.

One of the boys who grew up in the building was a sixteen- or seventeen-year-old kid named Shay, who wore two-carat studs in each ear. Whenever he saw Kalfani, he'd say, "Look hard, y'all! That boy there"—he'd point—"he's gonna make it to the NBA! Y'all can say you knew him when he was getting his game on, and you punk-asses were standing around here high as shit!"

Some of the boys' faces would harden with jealousy, while others, maybe because they were high, appeared giddy, others blank. I tried not to meet anyone's eyes because a glance can easily be mistaken for a stare, which pinpoints where 99 percent of beefing starts in the hood. But I agreed with Shay. Kalfani would make it to the top. And he would take his mother with him. No question there.

A Caribbean immigrant, Kalfani's mother, Mrs. Hogg, had at least two jobs: one cleaning houses across town in Bethesda and another subbing for in-home nursing aides. I rarely saw her, even when I spent the night, but her love of her kids was palpable and filled their home. There were always foil-covered plates of home-cooked food left for dinner, notes about doing homework, and brief phone calls to check in on Kalfani when we arrived home.

In time, I began to absorb Kalfani into my own being. I mimicked his confident stride. I hyped myself to "Ruff It Off," a go-go song by the Junkyard Band, which he'd introduced me to, before every game. With his encouragement, I approached a really cute girl at our school, and she didn't tell me to get lost. Eventually, most of the kids at school forgot about my white mother, whose appearance when she dropped me off would awkwardly put my biraciality on display. I was a young kid, struggling with the loss of my Nigerian heritage and my name, with my parents' divorce and my father's departure, and in its place, I found the belonging and acceptance that Kalfani's friendship and basketball granted me. Even the Rec Specs I wore after repeatedly breaking my glasses drew only occasional disses.

Late one afternoon, Kalfani walked me out of his apartment, and in the hallway, lingering on one of the landings, we encountered some of the older boys, including Shay. "Yo, there's my man," Shay said.

"Hey!" Kalfani gave and received the standard round of pounds and fist bumps as we headed down the stairs.

"Yo," Shay called after me, his voice deeper than I had ever heard it before. I kept walking.

"Yo," he said a second time. He wasn't addressing me; he was commanding me. I stopped on the stairs and pivoted toward him. Punk status awaited me if I didn't.

Shay's diamond studs gleamed as he squinted like a marksman, raising his thumb above his fist and stretching out his index finger in the shape of a gun. He aimed at the dead center of my pounding chest. My hands were down at my sides, but I felt them shake. I wanted to bolt but didn't dare move. I had to be able to look Kalfani in the eye again, so I had to hold steady. Shay broke into a wild laugh as he dropped his hand to his side. The other boys thought it was funny too.

"I'm just fucking with you," Shay said.

"William," Kalfani half pleaded, his feelings cut like a deck of cards. I was Kalfani's brother but so were these boys, and at that moment, they outnumbered me.

"Later," I said, facing down the stairs, mindful of the shadows at my rear and those that surrounded Kalfani, Shay, and the rest of the boys: gun violence, incarceration, premature death. What I would come to see years later is how that stairwell moment's awful eeriness foreshadowed Kalfani's tragic fate.

Things changed between Kalfani and me freshman year when my mother enrolled me in DC's prestigious St. John's College High School on scholarship, and we moved from urban Long Branch to the middle-class suburb of Beltsville, located in Prince George's County. For many Black boys, the transition from middle school to high school invites the lure of the hustle and street rituals that can beget violence. While I started playing high school basketball in a sheltered, racially integrated setting, Kalfani got to know the fundamentals of street life. Our daily basketball games became monthly hangouts, and eventually we saw each other just once or twice a year. Until we didn't see each other, period.

Still, I got the call.

"Kalfani is dead," Derrick, our mutual classmate and teammate on the basketball team at St. Michael's, said. "He got shot."

Kalfani wasn't the first or last person I knew who was lost to gun violence, but he was certainly the closest. I can recall his funeral only in nightmare-like fragments. Though I've long witnessed the impact of ubiquitous gun violence on the lives of young Black men, I came to recognize the depth of my own trauma and posttraumatic stress only when digging into my memory for this book. I was forced to confront how little I've been able to bear thinking about the murders of my childhood friends. The pain of their senseless deaths gives rise to a primal rage that, even now, I find difficult to manage. Why are Black boys worth so little when our potential is so enormous? Why do our society and culture tolerate the sight of our bodies left to bleed out on the street? Why do we, as Black boys and men, tacitly accept that for some of us killing each other simply seems like a brutal requisite for a doomed life?

I remember Kalfani was wearing a black suit and his hands were crossed at his waist. Mrs. Hogg sat in the pew, slumped over, looking off into the distance, devastated. I remember kneeling on the bench at the casket and praying for his soul and his mother. Struggling with difficult childhood memories has awakened me to how compassion for others can be traced back to the puncture wounds grief leaves in every one of us. Perhaps it was those spaces that made room in my heart for the mentorship of my seven Black fathers.

❖❖❖❖❖❖❖

Today I am living a life that neither Kalfani nor I could have imagined as children. I am a husband and a father, a civil rights attorney, an activist who has worked alongside Barack Obama, and an elected official in the great state of Maryland. As a Montgomery County councilmember, I represent more than a million people, a third of whom are foreign-born, in one of the most diverse counties in the nation.

Nearly fifteen years after Kalfani died, I discovered we were both part of a study we knew nothing about. Conducted by researchers at Harvard, Stanford, the Census Bureau, and the Internal Revenue Service, "Race and Economic Opportunity in the United States: An Intergenerational Perspective" tracked the income of the twenty million children born in America between 1978 and 1983 to examine why certain groups fare better economically than others. What the study found was just how much worse off Black boys and men are than everyone else.

For Black boys in the United States, wealth and family structure do not level the playing field. Our moms can be single parents or married. Our parents can be rich or poor. High levels of educational attainment matter less for us than they do for Black women, white women, and white men. Race and gender are such enormous and damning factors in the lives of Black men that the specific circumstances of our childhoods, our family backgrounds, our intelligence, actually do a lot less work and matter a lot less for us over the long haul of our lives than they do for every other group in this country. The statistic on Black male success is staggering. In 99 percent of census tracts in our nation, Black boys' outcomes were either stagnant or on a downward trajectory. That means in just 1 percent of the richest country in the world Black boys are on par with their white counterparts. Again, that's 1 percent.

Located in slivers of Queens and the Bronx in New York City and the Maryland Beltway suburbs where I'm from, these Black boy safe zones are different from the other 99 percent of census tracts in a distinct, measurable way. The 1 percent areas are populated with large numbers of working-class Black fathers. The Black boys who grow up in these places essentially come of age in a fairer America, where race and class don't inevitably torpedo their prospects.

The 2018 *New York Times* analysis of the "Race and Economic Opportunity" study said of 1 percent areas, "Poor black boys did well in such places, whether their own fathers were present or not." The Harvard sociologist William Julius Wilson stated it another way: "They're not talking about the direct effects of a boy's own parents' marital status. They're talking about the presence of fathers in a given census tract."

A father in the home matters to his Black son. And in these communities, a father in one home is potentially a mentor to a boy in another. I know that when I'm considered successful, I'm seen as a Black boy who transcended his circumstances. That's not the real story. I am who I am today exactly *because of my circumstances.* The single greatest difference between Kalfani and me during those critical adolescent years was the Black men that I gained access to because of my mother's job and where I went to school. These Black men—my mother's colleagues, certain teachers, my stepfather—taught me how to navigate the world and find my place in it. The Black men in my life made me, an emotionally fatherless boy, whole. And it was being made whole that enabled me to take full advantage of all the other opportunities that came my way, including a new story with my biological father, an emotionally present relationship with my children, and the ability to be a partner worthy of my wife. The power of these Black male mentors is that they make America a more just place for Black boys and a better place for *all* Americans.

My Seven Black Fathers tells the stories of the men who have shaped my sense of what it means to be a Black man in twenty-first-century America: Joseph Jacob, Mr. Williams, Jay Fletcher, Wayne Holmes, Deen Sanwoola, Barack Obama, and, ultimately, my own father, Olayinka Ishola Jawando. For Black men, having access to father figures can be the difference between a fulfilling life, or poverty, incarceration, and early death. In each chapter, I explore the distinct and indelible ways these men, my Black fathers, set me on the path of self-love, service, and wholeness.

My Seven Black Fathers retells the story of who Black fathers are. My seven Black fathers demonstrate there's no one right way to mentor and there's no standard fit.

My stepfather, Joseph Jacob, showed me, a broken child of

divorce, how to serve and love. My fourth-grade math teacher, Mr. Williams, saved me from two blights kids regularly face at school: bullying and racism. Jay Fletcher demonstrated to me that a man's strength has little to do with conventional notions of masculinity as I struggled with weight and body image. Wayne Holmes guided me through athletic disappointment by teaching me that failure is preparation for what's up next. Deen Sanwoola offered me a way back to my roots that ultimately helped me gain a relationship I'd run from all my life, one with my biological father. Barack Obama's vision of the possibilities of this nation, fatherhood, and brotherhood in America cleared a way for me to do the kind of mentoring of boys like Kalfani and myself that has been the bedrock of my adult life.

What my story proves is that the raw material of Black male success and wholeness is contained in the very bones of Black men. By having access to Black men who cared about me, who strove to help me succeed, who loved me even when I didn't understand what that meant, I became a statistic on the positive side of America's skewed racial balance sheet. I am convinced that, more than any other intervention, access to Black men who were willing to give of their time, wisdom, and compassion would have made a difference in Kalfani's life. On a micro level, mentorship has the potential to close the gap between a Black boy's aspirations and his potential. On a macro level, these Black men and their mentorship can help engineer social justice in the never-ending pursuit of a better America.

My journey of father loss, fathers found, and father healing is at the core of my moral vision for a healthy and vibrant community. I know that if I can be whole, my community can be healed. *My Seven Black Fathers* is my love letter to Black men. A missive to remind Black men that your life experience can have a profound and positive impact on the lives of Black boys, notwithstanding the challenges we will endure. Don't underestimate your role, your vulnerabilities, your past, and the power you hold in your own community. Own it. Wield it. Mentor.

To white people I say, this story is yours too. Black men have a complicated and challenging history in our country that has contributed to our strengths and some of our current poor outcomes. Give the lives of Black men and boys context and historical grounding. Do your part to relearn and retell the story of Black men in this country and in turn help to shape a new story about who America is. You can help enable mentoring relationships between Black men and boys through practices, policies, and programs. If you know a Black child that needs some guidance and have access to a Black man, introduce them. If you work in a school district, advocate for more Black male teachers when you have a decision maker's ear. If you are a school principal or superintendent, initiate a recruitment effort focused on hiring, supporting, and retaining Black men to work in elementary education. For those who are involved with youth organizations, like Girl Scouts or Boy Scouts, or are a coach or another kind of youth leader, try to build critical consciousness in the group by discussing inequities. What do we want for our collective future? I've thought about the answer to this question a lot in my work with My Brother's Keeper during the Obama administration, in my research on education, and in my current job as a Montgomery County councilmember. And what I keep coming back to is that I'm working for a future that's less like the past, a future where race and gender are less predictive of all our outcomes, especially those of Black boys.

By opening up about my relationships, I hope to break down the racist trope of the absent Black father while also telling a universal story of hurt, healing, and redemption. This book begins with my parents' divorce, and it ends with me taking care of my father at the end of his life. The redemption my father and I achieved is at the heart of who I am as a parent. The quest for wholeness that began with my father and led me to my mentors has taught me to unearth and cultivate facets of the relationships I have with my wife, my daughters, and my son, but also with dear friends and colleagues. This book is about Black men reaching out to heal one another, but it also provides a model for how to reach out to any young person. Or if you are the young person, how to accept help.

Finally, *My Seven Black Fathers* is a call to action. Can you imagine having a cure for someone suffering from a multisystem disease and not offering it to them? This disease is multisystem because of how it impacts the major organs of your life: your relationships, your finances, your physical and mental health. In the zip code where my mother worked and my parents eventually bought a home, the outcomes of Black boys are not as devastated by this disease as in most other places in America because the treatment for this catastrophic chronic illness is available. The multisystem disease is called racism. How you cure it in Black boys is with the presence of present, diverse Black men who are willing to step up and be mentors. To be "fathers." The rewards flow to us all.

1

JOSEPH JACOB

THERE ARE MANY PLACES TO BEGIN A STORY LIKE MINE, AND they are often sites of grief or mourning. Without the stone memorials placed in the ground to commemorate these sites, Black men like me carry the heavy markers of absence in our memories. Suitcases and the echo of slammed doors. Someone you love turning their back on you and walking away, getting smaller and smaller until they disappear and a piece of you disappears with them. That's how my father made me feel when I was a kid: like I missed something only he could give me.

As an only child, I recognized early that I was not alone in this; that I belonged to a brotherhood of boys and men who had lost their fathers. The distant expression, equal parts sorrow and wrath, that eddies in someone's eyes when they are accustomed to watching people walk away, or have walked away themselves, marked these men. Men in their prime, many of them in my working-class community, uniformed janitorial staff or postal workers, cooks or transit employees, exhausted from lives spent on shifts, announced that they saw themselves or their sons in me when they nodded in my direction or delivered me a muted smile while boarding a bus. I also got the nod from young men, teenagers really, sporting black Triple F.A.T. Goose coats or Starter jackets in the winter and wifebeaters in the summer, their strong brown chests adorned with gold rope chains and crosses, single cigarettes tucked behind ears, some of them wearing the most cherished status symbol of all: a pair of Jordans. These boys were my brothers and my father's too—my father whose own father had withheld love and attention from him. But rarely, if ever, did my father behold the world and see versions of himself or his experience in it. He wouldn't have been so guarded and distant if he had. The truth was that Dad, like so many wounded men, embraced his defenses and rejected his vulnerability. This choice made him weak. It takes vulnerability to love.

◆◆◆◆◆◆

In my earliest memories, my parents, Kathleen and Olayinka, are my whole universe. Mom would wake me up in the mornings by rubbing my back in a circular motion and whispering in my ear that she loved me today and every day. As I brushed my teeth and she applied her makeup in the bathroom mirror, she'd give me a quick scratch on my head or a caress behind my ear. We read Little Golden Books together in bed and she'd hum "Silent Night" as I fell asleep. Nestled under Mom's arm on the couch we watched *ThunderCats* and *He-Man* and even that ironic Disney cartoon where the Dickens character Scrooge gets a makeover as Scrooge McDuck, millionaire foster dad. While Mom prepared dinner, I'd play with my Batman and Robin action figures at her feet. She'd chime in with the only line she could recall from the sixties television show: "Holy crap, Batman!" I would laugh and laugh and Mom would too. Then my father would come home, and I would leap at him and wrap my arms around his legs and squeeze. He'd try to smile, but I felt him flinch. His day at work had made him raw.

A contract IT technician, Dad worked steadily at temp gigs, unable to land a permanent job. It felt like every week or two he'd start at a new place. The casual racism of his white managers kept them from learning his name, let alone how to pronounce it. He felt his accent hindered him, and it certainly did. The contempt he had to bury at work inflamed him at home. Every night I followed him from the front door into the living room, where he used the television or the stereo to erect a personal force field. I tried to penetrate it by standing next to him, or the television, or the stereo. He ignored me, either staring straight at the screen as if there weren't a small boy right beside it, or closing his eyes to listen to the Orchestra Baobab, the Senegalese jazz band from the sixties and seventies that sounded like a moody night in Havana. Eventually Mom would see what was happening and call me back to the kitchen, where a quiet would descend upon us. She tried to amuse me with another "Holy crap, Batman!" or something else in a funny voice, but now there was no laughter.

Dad had emigrated from Nigeria to study computer science in Kansas, graduated with a BS degree, and put one foot in front of the other. He held on to pieces of the American dream, like education and a marketable skill set, but the compensation and recognition that were supposed to come along with those pieces eluded him. He saw his own failure everywhere he looked. In our gritty neighborhood, in his paycheck, in the faces of his wife and child. The love my mother and I had for him could not give him the validation he sought from the outside world or even from the face he saw when he looked in the mirror. Mom had fallen in love with a brooding, passionate, complicated man, but the pressures of parenting recast Dad as a man unable to make peace with himself. He had imagined that he would be able to provide his family with what we needed, and the chasm between his expectations and our reality pained him. In that chasm, my father's idea of the American dream burned to ash. Even then some small part of me knew that I needed to find something, someone else to connect with before the flames enveloped me too.

Saturday mornings my father got up, got dressed, and went out alone. I begged him pretty please to take me with him, prayer hands and all, because he worked the rest of the week and I was in school. Nothing doing. I promised obedience. I promised to bag groceries at the supermarket like I had seen older boys do and give him my plastic cup of earnings at the end of every day. I promised to eat all my vegetables. But Dad flatly refused. Sometimes I'd hide his keys or his wallet to stall him, trailing him from room to room as he searched under magazines and newspapers and in between pieces of mail. Eventually Dad would find what I had hidden, and I'd start pleading again to go with him, jumping up and down at his side. "Please, please, let me come! Please!" He would just push me aside and leave in a hurry, as if I had made him late for something. Sometimes I'd stage tantrums that Dad would walk out on and leave my mother to deal with. Where did he go? What did he do when he went out? What did I do to make him leave? Mom would calm me with breakfast, help me get dressed, and we'd head to the park. Dad would arrive home in the afternoon and reclaim his place in the living room. Where he had gone remained a mystery.

One Saturday morning, after Dad predictably refused to take me with him, Mom and I went out shopping. It was early spring and the sun made me squint. I looked in the storefronts at our reflections in the glass, and past them at cashiers in friendly exchanges with customers. We turned onto University Boulevard, passing a Roy Rogers, the fried chicken place that bore the name of the old-time Hollywood cowboy star. A young woman outside with a bucket of sudsy water squeegeed the large pane of glass one long rectangle at a time, and the window went from mottled to clear. I stood still for a moment, captured by the simple beauty of a clean shining thing. Mom also stopped, but to dig in her purse for a tissue. Admiring the clean glass, I saw inside, at a booth . . . was it him? The man sat alone with a teacup, staring at a folded newspaper. It was Dad, sitting there alone. It was Dad. This was his secret. Sitting alone in Roy Rogers was his Saturday secret. Mom wiped her nose, reclaimed my hand, and the two of us continued down the street. He would rather be alone than with me, with us, I kept thinking. My head pounded so hard I could barely see. I told my mother I wanted to go home, and we did. I never told her, or my father, what I had seen. And I never again asked to go with him on a Saturday morning. My mother's love may not have shielded me from my father's rejection, but it kept me from being destroyed by it.

Dad did love us, though it was decades before I found that out. He just didn't see very much of himself in us to love. Mom is white and American, and it was hard for him to construe me as Nigerian in a foreign land without a Nigerian community to raise me in. Unlike my father, Mom had a job where she had authority and respect. She was production manager at a publishing firm specializing in policy newsletters for DC political insiders, but in my father's eyes, her success only further diminished him. My parents lacked the tools to understand their own feelings, much less express them or support each other. So, Dad's rage about Mom's success pushed him away from us and ultimately pushed Mom away from him.

One night at dinner, as sirens whined in the distance, my father sat in the living room with his legs spread wide, watching seventies reruns on TV. Mom tried to ignore him, taking the paper towel I had folded in half under her fork and putting it on her lap. "You do such a good job making things nice," she said with a smile. I liked setting the table. It was an easy way to make Mom happy. Dad glowered as he walked the few feet from the living room to the kitchenette table where we had all our meals.

"These are the things you teach him," he shouted. "The importance of keeping your mouth clean." He grabbed the folded paper towel from under his fork, opened it wide, and dabbed at the corners of his lips like he was doing pantomime. "How clean have you been keeping your mouth, Kathy? Tell me!" He stood and kicked his chair from behind him. "Tell me!"

My mother shook her head, tears streaming down her face. "I'm faithful," she said. "I'm not happy. But I'm faithful."

My father threw the chair into the hallway outside the kitchen. A wooden leg snapped and he stepped over it back into the living room. Mom let out a whimper and I wrapped my arms around her. We held each other for at least a minute in silence, our thoughts dominated by a man whose distance from us only drew us closer together.

As an immigrant, my father moved across the globe in pursuit of a better life. Like so many Black men in America, the circumstances that shaped him were ones he could not control: housing, employment, xenophobia, the absence of mentors. The combination of being supremely mobile but utterly stuck created an abysmal disappointment within my father. What sealed his perpetual unhappiness was that he considered a wife and child accessories to material success rather than their own reward.

Not long after he destroyed his own chair at the kitchen table, Dad moved out. Mom told him he had to leave, and he made no effort to stay. I resented that no one asked me what I wanted. But I'm not sure I could have answered if anyone did. I longed for my father's love, but I knew that expecting it was like flipping the switch on a light with a burned-out bulb.

Dad paid child support when he had it. But Mom couldn't rely on that so we moved to a smaller apartment in a worse part of Silver Spring. Lined with battered doors secured by three and four locks, the dark hallways smelled of cigarette smoke mixed with bouillon and bay leaves some days, and fried chicken and greens others. In our new vermin-infested home, the heat hissed and sprayed from radiators that peeled paint, or we wore sweaters over our pajamas when the boiler broke down. Comforted by each other's company, at first we experienced my father's absence as a loosening up, a release. Despite our living conditions, I remember this time as mostly happy. I say mostly because I still missed my father, and in the magical thinking mode that comes easily to anyone grieving, I believed we could be a family again. Dad's absence threw the pall of "if only" over my young life.

If only Dad had stayed, I wouldn't have been so afraid at night of the mice scratching behind the walls and of the roaches scattering across the floor when Mom turned on the light. If only Dad had stayed, we'd be living somewhere nice, beautiful even, in a house like on *The Cosby Show* or *Family Matters*. If only Dad had stayed, I wouldn't be the only Black person when Mom and I went to visit our family in Kansas. If only Dad had stayed, we could have visited Nigeria together. I could have seen with my own eyes the places he traveled to in his mind, heard with my own ears the voices he held in his heart, felt on my own skin my grandmother's embrace. If only Dad had stayed, I would have been able to know all that he came from, all that I come from. If only Dad had stayed, I would have been whole.

❖❖❖❖❖❖❖

Eventually Dad and I settled into a visiting routine. He picked me up around noon on Sundays and we would spend an interminable hour or so in the same Roy Rogers booth where he used to spend his coveted Saturday mornings. He had tea. I had hot chocolate and fries. He always brought *The Washington Post*, the big Sunday paper, a bulwark in case the conversation flagged, but even though it always did, he never opened the paper. He would stare into space, stare at the paper, stare at his hands, stare at just about anything but me. Soft rock and blue-eyed soul played on the staticky speakers.

"How's your mother?" Dad asked, looking away.

"Fine."

"You notice any new people around?"

"In the building?"

"No. I mean in your apartment, to visit. Any men?"

I shook my head. Why was he asking me this? Why would men visit the apartment? He never asked about me, just about my grades, perfunctorily, as if he were checking off a list. Bloated with the emptiness of it all—the food, his jealousy, his nonparenting—I shifted in the booth and fingered the fries. Just to have something to do I scarfed them down in two or three handfuls. Dad never once told me to slow down, asked me if I'd had enough or if I wanted something else.

Around this time, I attended kindergarten at a Black Catholic school called Nativity in the Brightwood neighborhood of DC. The teachers were nice, I liked the busy schedule, and since Mom worked until 5:00 p.m. she registered me for the aftercare program. A friend from work, a short, brown-skinned Black man named Joseph, came with her to the school one evening to pick me up. Joseph was the printer at her job. His car had refused to start, and Mom offered to take him home after she picked me up.

Joseph talked so much he hardly paused for breath. He asked how I was and what happened at school. He asked about my lunch and if I had suggestions for the chef. I giggled, and so did Mom, since she was the chef. The two of them chatted and Joseph kept pitching questions to me in the back seat. When Mom inquired where to drop Joseph off, it turned out that he lived only a few blocks away from us.

After that, Joseph was always around. We window-shopped at the mall and went out to eat with him. He chaperoned me at arcades and at the park. On Saturdays, when Joseph ran errands, Mom encouraged me to tag along. He would drop off cleaning, bring this or that to the post office. Big hellos and boisterous little conversations greeted him everywhere. A strange shyness came over me around these new people, strange because I wasn't shy, and I was enjoying myself in Joseph's company. I just couldn't stop thinking about how different he was from Dad. My father had left his country behind, and seemed adrift. Joseph was so at home in his country that just strolling around and running errands brought him joy. I couldn't help liking Joseph's way better, but hearing myself have the thought made me feel bad, like I was betraying Dad.

Joseph shared a small duplex with his older brother Raymond on Eleventh Avenue, a house their mother had left them when she died. Whenever Mom and I went over there, his brother popped in with news about a neighbor or just to say hello. Joseph taught me to play cards, and over the course of our games he would regale me with stories about how much DC had changed since he was a kid and how young people today weren't what they used to be, with their rap music, baggy pants, and Ebonics. I tried to understand what he was saying, but it didn't make a lot of sense to me at the time. What I did understand was just how much time Joseph was spending with us.

One night I got up to use the bathroom after I had been asleep for a few hours. When I finished, the sound of the TV drew me to the living room. There on the couch, in the blue light of our ancient Zenith, Mom and Joseph were kissing. I tiptoed back to bed and lay there, as wide-awake as I'd ever been. This is what my father had been talking about. This is what Dad had dreaded. Seeing it with my own two eyes, I finally understood. Dad hadn't asked for ages if there had been any men around, mainly because he had missed so many visits and was hardly around himself. But now there *had* been a man around. And it wasn't Dad.

One warm Saturday, as we were strolling from the drug-store to the post office, Joseph put his hand on my shoulder. "I've been thinking," he said, very casually, as if he were deciding between hot dogs or hamburgers. "I want us to be a family."

My thoughts raced. Was kissing my mother in a way I had seen no one kiss her before, ever, not even my father, proof of how much Joseph wanted to be a family? Was that how people made the leap from friend to family? With open-mouthed kisses?

I gave him a side-eye. "How exactly would that work?"

"Well, your Mom and I could get married." He had clearly given this some thought.

"I don't know," I said. "Mom's already done that."

Joseph laughed. "She could do it again. And you know what? I've *never* been married."

"There a reason for that?" I asked.

Thinking about it now, a little kid asking that question, Joseph could easily have kept laughing or changed the subject. But he didn't. He looked me directly in the eye. "I've never loved anyone like I love you and your mother," he said.

His declaration was so pure and simple, it went straight to my heart. Those words were everything I'd always wanted to hear from my father and suddenly I hated Joseph for saying them. I hated Joseph for not being my father. I hated my father for being the way he was, and not like Joseph. I hated my father for not being proud of me like Joseph was. And I hated myself for loving Joseph back.

At the end of kindergarten, the school had me take some kind of test. My score suggested that I could skip first grade, and my mother agreed. On Saturday errands with Joseph, that was all he could talk about for weeks. "You see li'l man here," Joseph said. "He's getting skipped from kindergarten to second grade!" Folks clapped at the barbershop and congratulated me at the pharmacy with a chorus of "Go on, now!" "You so smart!" and "Look at you! You doing big, big things, young man!" Like any kid, I enjoyed being singled out for my intelligence; I liked thinking I was smart; I liked other people thinking it, too. More nervous than she let on about my transition from being a kindergartner at a Black school to a second grader at a white school, Mom did what she could to ensure I made the adjustment.

There was another adjustment to be made. "You're starting a new school." Mom smiled. "That's an opportunity for a new start." I was listening closely. "One way to start fresh is with a new name."

I was confused. "A new name?"

"Yes," Mom answered. "And you have one. Your first name, William."

"My name is Yemi, short for Opeyemi," I answered matter-of-factly, because my name for the first six years of my life had been a matter of fact.

"Actually," Mom said, "Opeyemi is your second name. William is your first name. I gave it to you after an uncle of mine who passed. He was a wonderful man. He would have loved you."

I was still trying to wrap my head around having two names,

not to mention an uncle I'd never met who would have loved me even though he was dead, when Joseph added, "It's time for a new start, William."

I looked at them both sideways. "Did the school say I need a new name to go there?"

"No," Mom said. "But I think the name William will make things easier for you."

"What do you mean, easier? What's easier about 'William'?" Was a name going to make it easier to do math, or write in cursive? Was it going to help me learn how to play basketball?

Joseph knelt down to look straight at me. "The thing is, William doesn't sound African . . . like Yemi. Your teacher told your mom about the kids making fun of your name."

I didn't know the teacher had noticed, let alone told my mom. But it was true. Some of the kids in kindergarten called me Yummy. I thought it was because I was chubby, but it hit me that they wouldn't have called me that if they had known me as William. I didn't understand then that when my mom and Joseph said *easier* they meant less African, more American.

I wondered how my father would take the name change. Sometimes I thought Dad was deliberately cruel—I figured he couldn't be so hurtful to us without wanting to be. Other times, like when he skipped Sunday visit after Sunday visit, I thought it was pure indifference—he didn't even care enough to call and say he wasn't coming. Whatever the reason, Mom rejected Dad's treatment of us and got a divorce. Now, with Joseph at her side, she also rejected Dad's name for me. Mom walked me through rejecting it too. At the door, in the morning, just before we headed out for the day, I heard her saying sweetly, *Your name is William now.* The night before, Mom standing at the stove while I set the table, saying sweetly, *Your name is*

William now. I warmed to the idea because it represented a departure from my father, not from Blackness. Far from thinking about my mother as a white American and my father as a Black Nigerian, I focused on the way each of them loved me. My mother's love was warm, soft, undeniable. My father's was a variable, a moving target, always in question. Looking back, I see that my name became a proxy for my identity, the territory on which each of my parents staked their claim. For Mom and Joseph, the name Yemi belonged to my father. As William, I belonged to them.

A lot of the kids I grew up with carried their mothers' last names. My mother actually kept my father's name, Jawando, because she wanted our claim to each other in the bureaucratic world of applications and forms to be airtight. Mom also made peace with our last name as her acknowledgment of Dad's importance despite the fact that they'd divorced. And despite her feelings about him, she wanted me to know that no matter what, he would always be my father.

Whenever Joseph picked me up from school, folks assumed he was my biological father and called him Mr. Jawando. Joseph, always comfortable in his skin, never minded. Part of me resented people calling Joseph by my father's name because it was Joseph who showed up for me, not Dad. Another part of me breathed a deep sigh of relief simply because Joseph was Black. If my mother had chosen a white man, to the outside world, I would have looked like an outsider in my own family.

◆◆◆◆◆◆◆

Mom and Joseph exchanged office gossip in the evenings while they cooked together and brainstormed ideas for work projects.

One evening, Mom stood at the kitchen sink when Joseph came up behind her and wrapped his arms around her waist. "My apartment is so much nicer than this," he said, pointing at the dingy kitchen and outdated appliances. "Come on. It'll work. We'll be able to save money. Let's get married."

It wasn't the first time I had heard Joseph propose but this time Mom turned, wrapped her arms around his neck, and buried her head in his chest. It was going to happen.

Mom and Joseph got married on a bright August morning. In the first suit jacket I can remember wearing, complete with a carnation pinned to the lapel, I served as their witness at the courthouse in Rockville, where I now work across the street as a county councilmember. It felt very formal and official, but something prevented me from signing off on my new relationship to Joseph. That something was my father.

As Joseph became more and more a part of my life, Dad's visits with me became more and more frequent. Dad still didn't think to ask what I was doing or how I was doing, but he had a new theme to break up the awkward silences that swelled between us as we sat across from each other at the same sticky table. In the same voice he would use for something as banal as "Put on your seatbelt," he would say, "Joseph stole your mother from me, Yemi. Joseph destroyed our family." He'd take a sip of his tea, put the cup down, and stare. Then he would say, "Joseph will leave you and your mother, Yemi. Mark my words: He will leave."

As soon as he'd drop me off at home, I would lie on the couch, sick with his suspicions. I would retch over the bathroom sink, but nothing ever came up. Mom and Joseph talked about what to do. They took me for tests that turned up nothing. Mom also took me to a counselor but found the office too sterile and the therapist too cold to return. While Mom and Joseph tried to figure out how to help me, they were also newlyweds who hadn't been on a honeymoon. As we readied ourselves to go out on errands one Saturday, Joseph asked what I thought about him and Mom going away on their own for a week. Dad was right, Joseph *was* going to leave, but he wasn't leaving Mom and me—he was leaving me and taking Mom with him. "You're a thief, Joseph! My father was right! You ruined our family! You stole Mom from Dad! And now you want her all to yourself! But she's *my* mother! Mine!" I yelled again and again.

Joseph tried to calm me down. "I didn't steal anyone," he said. "I love you. You are my family."

Mom tried to hold me. "Joseph couldn't steal me," she said. "I'm not an object. I'm a person. You can't steal a person. No one will ever be able to steal me from you, William. Ever."

I broke away and faced Joseph again. "Why do you think you're better than my father? You're not! You'll leave, too! You'll leave us, just like he said!"

Joseph knelt in front of me. Firmly, lovingly, he held my shoulders, even as I tried to twist away.

"I'm not leaving you," he said. "Even if your mother and I broke up, which we're not going to do, I wouldn't go anywhere. You're my son too now. And I love you."

I challenged him. "I'm *your* son?"

"Yes, you're my son, William."

"You're not going to leave?"

"No. Not ever."

I cried hard, then harder as Joseph held me. Soon Mom joined the huddle and the three of us watered our roots as a family. Joseph's declaration that night finally inoculated me against my father's warped claims. It also inoculated me against a misguided claim of my own, that Joseph loved me only because I was my mother's son.

◆◆◆◆◆◆◆

A DC native, Joseph Walker Jacob was born in the Freedmen's Hospital in May 1961. Founded almost exactly a hundred years before Joseph's birth, in 1862, the Freedmen's Hospital was the first healthcare facility established in the United States to care for and serve free Black people. The hospital also became a platform for the effort to free and train Black minds through education. In 1868, when the facility joined with Howard University, it became one of the first teaching hospitals in the nation where Black medical school students could receive instruction. If you were to ask Joseph where he was born he'd answer plainly and with great pride, "The Freedmen's Hospital in Washington, DC." Joseph might not tell the history I've just shared with you, but he'd want you to know it.

Joseph remembers his days as a kid passing in a blur of wholesome structure: school, playground, television, dinner, bedtime. From 1964 through 1967, race rebellions broke out in Watts, Detroit, Chicago, Philadelphia, and Newark, but all that seemed far away from his well-ordered life. Then tragedy struck. In 1968, when Joseph was seven years old, an assassin's bullet murdered Martin Luther King Jr.

Dr. King was shot on a balcony at the Lorraine Motel in Memphis, Tennessee, on the evening of Thursday, April 4. The next day at the Lucretia Mott Elementary School, where Joseph was a second grader and his mother, Jacqueline, worked as a first-grade teacher, the principal issued an early dismissal. The way Joseph tells it, sirens shrieked nonstop. He lived on Fourth and Bryant Streets in the northeast section of the city, for the most part a residential neighborhood. A Safeway, a liquor store, and a cleaners operated near the row house where Joseph lived with his parents and two older brothers. The boys stared out the living room windows at the unusual activity. "Dozens of people walked in the street on our normally quiet block. Others lingered, not exactly up to anything. The energy was electric. My brothers and I wanted to go outside. Mom forbade us, so we settled for watching," Joseph recounted. "Suddenly, the mood shifted. Looting had started. People ran through the street with arms full of dry cleaning. Others pushed shopping carts overflowing with food. Some changed course, threw down the dry cleaning, and headed off in the direction of the grocery store. Smoke started to roll in. Soon, it was going to be hard to see anything. My father may not have needed permission to go outside but he needed an excuse. He had one: the trash. He sidled out the door and returned a few minutes later carrying a case of liquor he had discovered alongside the rubbish bins in the alley. My mother lost it. Why would he claim something that was stolen? What kind of example did he expect to set for us boys? My father shrugged. The alcohol was free. He would have been a fool to leave it. A fool? My mother hammered back. These Black folks, many of them teenagers, running around like chickens with their heads cut off, stealing what they didn't earn! *Those people* were the fools. What had Dr. King died for? For Black people to have an excuse to destroy themselves and their communities for the thrill of it? Dr. King dedicated his life to the improvement of Black people. He was dead now. These people in the streets acted like Dr. King's dream was dead too. Mom stopped there. Not much more could be said or heard above the sirens anyway."

The riots lasted four days. The Northeast, Northwest, and Anacostia neighborhoods were burned beyond recognition. Joseph had witnessed the frenzied lawlessness outside his home. He had listened to his parents argue. His mother felt let down by Black people. His father had never expected much from Black people, or people of any race for that matter. Joseph embraced his mother's perspective. Blackness came to be defined as one of two things for Joseph: the cause of self-regard or the reason for stigma. As a Black boy in elementary school, unsure of where I fit in the world, the clarity of Joseph's thinking was reassuring.

In second grade at the majority-white Our Lady of Lourdes Catholic School in upscale Bethesda where I went by William, kids touched my hair and asked if my skin was brown all over. I tried to ignore this when it happened, but afterward, contempt for the offending peer and humiliation at being singled out would congeal into anger. I told myself I should be able to brush it off, but I never could. Instead, I tried to bury my feelings by being a model student. Once, in third grade, I eagerly raised my hand to answer a question. Sure, I lifted my rear out of the seat. Sure, my volume rose when I pleaded, "Call on me! Call on me!" The white boy next to me did the same thing. Only the teacher called on him, and sent me to the principal's office.

Principal Smith opened the door of her office, and ushered me in with her eyes. She closed the door behind me and I took my seat in front of her desk, where the papers gathered into neat stacks looked like a game board. As she took her seat, Principal Smith's small stinging blue eyes bored into me. She folded her hands and planted them in front of her at the midway point between us. I utilized the only armor I had and folded my arms over my chest. When she spoke, only her mouth moved, nothing else.

"The teacher will choose who to call on, William. If you really want to learn, you will stop being disruptive. Disruptions to learning cannot be tolerated. Not here."

"But I wasn't disrupting! I raised my hand!" Mom had always said that I had my own soapbox. The urge to stand on it and shake my finger at this woman unnerved me mainly because I knew it was the right thing to do, but that the right thing would only get me in more trouble.

"Your teacher said you were being disruptive. Are you calling her a liar?"

"No . . ." I felt the tears coming but stopped them before they fell. Principal Smith gave me detention and dismissed me. I understood my offenses: enthusiasm, eagerness, and a desire to be acknowledged for something positive—all qualities that were encouraged and rewarded in my white peers but discouraged and penalized in me. Reliving this episode to write about it, one of the many things that disturbs me about my time at this school, in light of the principal's reprimand, is how my peers casually disrupted *my* learning. The obstacle and challenge the other children posed by taunting me with their ignorance was overlooked and disregarded. My competing with a white child to answer a question, though—that was noticed and punished.

If I had dared continue to argue my case to Principal Smith that day, I almost certainly would have been suspended, a type of discipline documented to be disproportionately used to punish Black children at egregious rates, especially in the younger grades. For too many Black kids in this country, the insidiousness and prevalence of racism whittles our responses down to either shut up or talk back, believe a lie or be punished for telling the truth, run or freeze—at school, in our neighborhoods, and on public transportation. For the rest of third grade, I didn't altogether stop being my busy, inquisitive self. But if you had asked me how I felt back then, I would have answered "sad." The expectation that Black children "behave" in classrooms rather than learn or participate in a meaningful way was inescapable. At the end of third grade, a time in a child's life when their reading proficiency can predict their success in school going forward, Principal Smith told Mom she should either put me on Ritalin or withdraw me from school. Mom withdrew me. She wasn't going to let them give me medicine I didn't need, and since I hated taking medicine, like most kids, that sounded good to me. At home, Joseph educated me on what it meant to be a Black child and how to survive. I had just turned eight.

All parents give their children talks shaped by broad factors like that child's race, culture, and gender. Joseph talked a lot with me about my third-grade teacher and Principal Smith. How he instructed me to act with them—stay polite, stay calm, show deference—is sadly similar to how Black parents instruct their children to interact with the police. For many children, myself included, racist encounters can devour a childhood. To lessen the chance that these encounters will destroy more than a childhood, generations of Black parents have taken their children's bodies into their own hands, and beaten them, out of fear. Tough discipline at home was delivered with the intention of keeping a child intact out in the world, a world where white supremacy infects how we raise our own children. I sometimes got mouthy with Joseph and was a smartass. An old-school Black parent and a believer in "spare the rod, spoil the child," Joseph did hit me sometimes to make a point that was for my own benefit. I don't discipline my children by beating them, and couldn't imagine ever doing that, but I understand the roots of that behavior. I also refuse to inspire my Black children by using white people as a standard, which is more old-school African American parenting, another go-to of Joseph's.

For generations Black folks have urged their children to deal with centuries-old, systemic bias in the "twice as good" speech. Joseph gave this speech to me basically from the time he started dating my mom, and I know Joseph's mother preached it to him. To be considered a success, in any endeavor, and to be properly acknowledged for your efforts, the speech goes, you need to work twice as hard and be twice as good as your closest white competitor. Whenever Joseph talked about his childhood, he told me about assemblies he attended at Lucretia Mott where passages were read aloud from manuals with the word *Negro* in the title that had been developed solely for an audience of "Negro" children. Ironically, the topic was self-control, at a time when white adults were lynching Black children in America. The curriculum would inevitably state how every Black girl and boy should strive to represent their race, their church, and their family as honest, upstanding, and reputable people. Faith, family, community, and service are the pillars of my life today. Joseph raised me up in this ethos. Yet, I've absorbed it with a bit more Black liberation than white preachiness guiding me.

Joseph's politics emerged, in part, from what he perceived as the flaws of Black people. I understand it as a response to American pathology. As a kid, I was very competitive—in school, in basketball. I still am. However, when I consider the "twice as good" ethos in the context of an American society engineered to assist white people with housing, employment, education, and health care—while knowing this same society has been designed to harm or neglect Black people in those same areas—I think aspects of respectability politics actually disrespect reality. Sometimes while listening to Joseph talk about the way "Negro" children were trained to have dignity and show respect, I would think about how the standard for Black people was perfection, while the standard for white people was merely to be human.

After his parents divorced, Joseph moved to Silver Spring with his mother, who raised him in the African American paradigm of parenting. Joseph followed in his mother's footsteps and parented me with his presence and example. He knew how to keep a family together and a household running. Joseph taught me how to repair a wobbly stool, how to service my own bike, how to mow a lawn efficiently, how to cut wood without throwing my shoulder out or hurting someone. These are simple skills, but they are important. What makes them important is that they require discipline, focus, and effort. What I learned from Joseph is that when these kinds of things are done right, often no one notices, but when they're done badly, or not at all, they create real problems. Being essential, especially to a child, isn't about social standing; it's about standing beside that child when they need you. Joseph did that work every day.

As my third parent, Joseph broke the spell of my white American–Black Nigerian binary with the presence of a Black American identity. The more comfortable I became in my African American identity, the less I took issue with Yemi and William. Though each of my natural parents had named me, neither of them could help me forge what was missing. That was what I inherited in large part from Joseph: my Black American identity.

❖❖❖❖❖❖❖

Mom had offered to drop me off at Dad's place for my Sunday visits with him after we had moved to Joseph's family's home, but he declined the offer. I could easily see why. A graffiti cloud of tags and obscenities covered the door to the lobby of his building. Young men flanked its entrance. Some of these same young men played dice and smoked weed in the stairwells, much as they had in Kalfani's building. Bowed by shame, and shoved around by his pride, Dad wanted to hide his life from Mom. This made him more likely not to show up for our visits, and if I waited a half hour on the stoop where Mom and I had moved in with Joseph and his brother, Dad wasn't coming.

Mom thought putting me in a soccer league would help offset the stress of the Sunday visits. Practices were after school and matches were on Sundays. Dad agreed to pick me up earlier for our visits and then take me to my match when our visit was done. When everything went as planned, Mom and Joseph stood at one end of the spectator section, and Dad at the other. At the end of the games, win or lose, Dad would wave goodbye from the sidelines. Mom and Joseph met me on the field, hugged me no matter how I'd played, and took me home. On the Sundays Dad didn't show, Mom would come outside with my soccer bag. She and Joseph would take me to the match, cheer me on, and bring me home. But my father's absence would loom, almost like he was sitting in the living room where I lived now with Mom and Joseph, silently watching television or nodding his head to his music, reminding me that he preferred doing nothing to being with me.

I waited and waited for Dad one Sunday. Then something unusual happened. Instead of Mom coming out to the stoop with my soccer bag, Joseph came outside empty-handed. He sat down beside me. For a long time, neither of us spoke.

"Why didn't you bring my soccer bag?" I asked.

"Do you even like soccer?"

"Not really."

"Why don't you tell your mother?"

"She wants me to do it."

"She wants you to be happy," Joseph said.

"Is that why she sent you out here?"

"She didn't send me."

"Then why are you here?"

"I want to talk to you about something."

"What?"

"Have you ever heard me say a bad word about your father?"

I stopped to think. "No."

"When I was a kid, after my father left, whenever he took me out he had a mean, cutting thing to say about my mother. But nothing he said changed the way I looked at my mother. It only changed the way I looked at him."

"How?"

"His petty hate was more important to him than my love for my mother. He was selfish. It made me angry."

"Are you still angry at him?" I asked.

"No."

"Why not?" I asked. I couldn't imagine forgiving anyone who trashed my mother.

"My father changed. He apologized. Olayinka could change too. He could apologize one day. The way things are now is not the way they have to stay. Nothing is forever. Not even this hostility between you and your father."

Joseph's words gave me hope—not that my father would change, but that *I* could change. That I could stop being angry at him. Unable to say any of this, or quite understand all that I was feeling, I went quiet. But that day Joseph planted in me the seed that many years down the road made something wondrous possible.

"Since you don't really like soccer, how about we change it up today," Joseph said.

"Change it up how?"

"Let's go to the movies," he said. "We'll get some popcorn and have ourselves a very good time."

◆◆◆◆◆◆

After that first Sunday at the movies where we saw flicks like *House Party 2* and *Teenage Mutant Ninja Turtles*, whenever my father didn't show, that's what Joseph and I did: we went to the movies, just the two of us. Driving home from the theater one night, Joseph gave me a strange look. His vulnerability shone brightly beneath his bravado. "I've got news for you, William." The preamble evidenced his nerves and got mine going. "From now on you're going to call me Sir, Mr. Jacob, or Dad. But you will not call me Joseph anymore." Whether I showed him respect in the mode of a stranger with "Sir," as a subordinate with "Mr. Jacob," or as his son with "Dad" was entirely up to me.

"Thanks for the notice, Mr. Jacob," I said, unwilling to submit. Nothing more about it was said that night.

Weeks of me calling him Mr. Jacob passed. I even tried Sir for a few days. I enjoyed teasing Joseph by being formal, extra respectful. I shared my life with him. I shared my mother with him. But the child in me did not want to share the name Dad with him, either because of the bad associations the word brought to my mind or because I didn't want to disrespect my real father.

Then a funny, offhand correction I offered said more about what I felt than I knew. Joseph had taken me to a doctor's appointment, and the receptionist addressed him as "Mr. Jawando," which happened all the time. "No," I told her. "This isn't Mr. Jawando. This is my dad." The receptionist blinked at me, then nodded. The end of an epoch had arrived. I called Joseph Dad from that point forward.

2

MR. WILLIAMS

RACING AROUND THE PLAYGROUND AFTER HOURS SITTING IN the classroom, I crashed into another kid's shoulder, knocking him back a step. A second grader in size six shoes, I was a big kid, but it was completely innocent. That didn't stop the playground monitor from snatching me by the arm, like I had premeditated an assault. When I asked to use the restroom, my teacher said to stop with the excuses. When I said the board was blurry, she accused me of not paying attention.

Had a white kid bumped into a classmate on the playground, it would have been an accident. And there would have been no shame in asking to use the bathroom. A white kid wouldn't have had to squint at the board from the back of the room. Had I been a white boy, I would have been appreciated for being outgoing and forthright, smart, a go-getter. Instead, where I was concerned, white teachers and administrators at the Catholic school I attended for second and third grade just wanted me out, and they cared little if they had to break me to do it.

From seven to eight years old, humiliation at school buckled my self-esteem. Alone, I thought about how I couldn't do anything right at school. At school, I yearned to be alone. It felt physically draining to sit in rooms where I was either surveilled or ignored. What I learned at school, day after day, was that I was a problem I had no idea how to solve, even as my teachers' instructions played on an endless loop: *Not now. Put down your hand. Be quiet.* Repetitive chastisement narrows us, saps us of joy and potential by ceaselessly reminding us how little is possible. And no matter how much we feel the treatment is unjust and undeserved, we inevitably internalize it over time. We cut ourselves down because we begin to accept the argument that something must be wrong with us. Not with the context, or the school, or the teacher, or the curriculum, but with us—within our very being.

The defenses many Black boys and girls employ to survive, like withdrawal and defiance, at first provide cover for our hopes and dreams, but those same coping mechanisms dull our personal aspirations. Spiritual amputation becomes the norm. This state of dejection, misery, and anger nearly enveloped me. Until a Black man named Mr. Williams came on the scene. It was Mr. Williams who saved me.

❖❖❖❖❖❖❖

I attended preschool and kindergarten at a Black school in DC called Nativity Catholic Academy, where everyone still knew me as Yemi, my Nigerian name. I skipped first grade and spent second and third grade at Our Lady of Lourdes, where my mother made sure I was known as William. I started fourth grade at my third school, Oak View Elementary School. Sensing it was unlikely to be the charm, I just wanted to make it through without being called out all the time. Then Mr. Williams walked into the classroom on my first day at Oak View Elementary.

Oak View was a majority Black and brown school in my Long Branch neighborhood of Silver Spring, Maryland, and many of the kids had been together since kindergarten. Everyone knew one another. I didn't know anyone, and I could tell no one wanted to know me in my no-name Payless sneakers and thick glasses.

Tall, brown-skinned, and handsome in the Morgan Freeman mold, Mr. Williams walked into the room carrying a faded black briefcase that despite its wear still looked expensive. He elegantly draped his navy blazer over his shoulder. Against the backdrop of his crisp white shirt, his richly colored burgundy tie reminded me of Christmas. I did a double take. Could this person be the teacher? I had never had a Black male teacher before. There had never been someone who looked like me at the head of the classroom. This was the first Black man I could ever remember seeing inside any school I attended, and wearing a tie, no less.

The man placed his briefcase on the desk and his blazer over the chair. He briefly put his hands in his pockets and vetted the class with a gaze of cool, contained professionalism. Most of the class, maybe thirty kids, instantly stopped the chitchat. He wrote his name on the blackboard in block letters and underlined it.

"I'm Mr. Williams," he said, returning the chalk to the tray, "your math teacher." He dusted his hands off on each other. "It's time I find out who all of you are. When I call your name please respond 'present' or 'here.'" Mr. Williams popped open his briefcase and removed a set of attendance cards. As he took the cards out of the rubber band, I sat nervously waiting for my name to be called. It was William now, not Yemi.

"William Jawando," Mr. Williams said, with the perfect enunciation of my distinctly West African last name, another first for me, in his clear baritone. Accented with a trace of the South, his voice had a smidge of a radio announcer in it.

I raised my hand eagerly. "Here!"

In so many ways, as a father and in my work as an activist

and public servant, Mr. Williams remains a presence in my life today. His dignity, his commitment to high standards and to carrying out those standards humanely, with great attention and care, are signposts that I employ regularly to guide my path. Yet, I never saw him outside of school, never laid eyes on him after the end of fourth grade, or even learned his first name, which demonstrates something important about mentorship. Mentors don't have to be involved in every aspect of someone's life to make a difference. Nor do mentors have to be a constant presence to have a deep impact. In just nine months, Mr. Williams changed my life with his.

◆◆◆◆◆◆◆

Mom had attended Catholic school from kindergarten through high school, and she wanted that discipline for me as well. She had always emphasized the value of the character education she received back in Kansas, how it had made her a woman with the inner strength to follow her heart wherever it led, even if it guided her light-years away from the white-bread life her parents had imagined for her. It was Catholic school that empowered my mother to keep her own counsel and make her own way.

Without my father's input, she'd decided to enroll me in Catholic school for early childhood education. My performance and test scores demonstrated that I was a bright-enough kid, and without Joseph's two cents, Mom had decided they would incur the financial cost of sending me to Our Lady of Lourdes. Painfully aware of how the divorce had affected me, and feeling guilty about it, Mom wanted to make up for it by giving me every opportunity to succeed.

"William, I want the best for you, including the best

school," she said, sitting on the edge of the bed to tuck me in. "You deserve the best. The best deserves you."

"Tomorrow is a big day," said Joseph. "The first day of school always is, but you're a big boy. You're ready for it." Joseph had my number. He could tell I was nervous. My first day at Lourdes was to be my first time out in the world as William. It was also going to be my first time in a majority-white space, outside of my mom's family in Kansas, where we spent most Christmas holidays. When Mom had brought me to visit Lourdes in the spring after we received the acceptance, I spied a few other brown faces in the higher grades, but none in the lower ones. The tricked-out homes in suburban Bethesda with pools and professional gardens, ponds and horse stables, many of them belonging to DC power brokers, sat mere miles from our neighborhood of modest apartments and duplexes in diverse Silver Spring, but Bethesda felt a world away. Joseph tried to prepare me for the journey between that world and mine and back again.

"There's a lot of talk at this school about how accepting and open-minded everyone is," Joseph explained. "That's good because a lot of places don't even bother to say that. But rich white folks don't tend to know a lot of people who look different from them. For that matter, they don't tend to know how to treat folks who look different from them either."

That made no sense to me. "How come?" I asked. Did having a lot of money mean you didn't have to act right by people who didn't have money? I started to think about it. Did we live where we did because we didn't know people who lived in nicer neighborhoods? Was knowing rich people the way to get rich?

Joseph smiled at my questions, but he didn't laugh. "What I'm trying to say is most of the rich folks are white folks, and money and manners don't always go together. That's just the way it is. This is a great school, but I don't want you to be taken by surprise *when* it happens, not *if* it happens." I heard the certainty in Joseph's voice.

His perspective wasn't always easy to hear but it was always worth listening to. Mom seconded his opinion with her silence and kissed me on the forehead. We exchanged good nights and I went to sleep.

❖❖❖❖❖❖❖

My second-grade teacher, Sister Antoinette, was a middle-aged woman who had spent decades abroad doing missionary work. She ran a quiet, orderly classroom with colorful bulletin boards devoted to literacy, math, and the seasons, supplying good cheer to the classroom. School had been in session for a few weeks, but I hadn't made any friends yet. One afternoon during recess, as I played by myself on the monkey bars, a child from another class ran up to me. He had spiky brown hair and green eyes. Did this boy want to be my friend? He would be the first.

"Hi," I said. The boy gawked. His two front teeth peered out of his mouth like some thought or question had pried his lips apart. Two or three years younger than this kid, I had almost a full two inches on him. "Hi," I said again. A moment later, the boy slapped my bare forearm. Open-mouthed and mute, he examined his palm. I thought I had been tagged because the spiky-haired boy tore off running. I followed. But the boy's voice stopped me cold in my tracks.

"It doesn't wipe off!" he said, holding up his hand to three or four other kids. The friends absorbed the news and quickly resumed their play. Wipe off? I thought anxiously, examining my forearm. No, nothing was on it. Then, it hit me. He was talking about my skin. These boys wondered if the brown of my skin would rub off on them.

That night at home, I wanted to tell Mom and Joseph what happened, but I couldn't bring myself to do it. I understood how important the school was to Mom. How much it cost. How badly she wanted me, her William, to succeed there. I wanted to succeed there too, more than anything. The next time I saw my father I considered telling him what had happened, but then thought better of it. Would he turn what some kid said on Mom and make it out to be her fault? Or would he just look down or stare at me silently, making that fleeting moment on the playground that much worse? I decided it wasn't worth finding out, so I kept it to myself.

On Monday mornings, after the Lord's Prayer and the Pledge of Allegiance, Sister Antoinette asked the class about our weekend. Hands shot up with mentions of lake houses and fishing trips, attendance at NFL games and shopping at Tysons Corner, a high-end mall in Northern Virginia. After winter break, a girl told the class she had traveled to Aspen for a ski holiday. I thought maybe aspirin came from Aspen for no other reason than the words sounded similar. After spring break, a boy excitedly shared that he swam with dolphins in the Bahamas. I swam in envy. On my school vacations, I hung out at the office with my parents in downtown Silver Spring, where I read and did crosswords in the conference room, or bounced between cubicles asking my parents' colleagues annoying questions.

While other families went on swanky vacations, mine worked. While other kids spent their weekends being shuttled from one pricey pastime to another, I ran errands with Dad on Saturday and sat in a Roy Rogers booth with my father on Sundays. Only my shame about that could compete with my envy. How drab my experiences were compared to my classmates', and the fact that they existed mostly within the scope of my neighborhood humiliated me. I never raised my hand to recount my weekend, share where I had gone on vacation, or say what I had done there. Besides, Sister Antoinette never called on me. Was she trying to spare me embarrassment? There are 175 school days, or forty school weeks, a year. Forty weeks of being ignored, of the weight of the assumption that I had nothing worth sharing with my classmates, wore on me. I kept it to myself.

Overall, that year in Sister Antoinette's class was successful academically. The decision to skip a grade had turned out to be sound. Strict but fair, Sister Antoinette was a good teacher. I worked hard; I did well. She encouraged me and I even received an award for outstanding performance in math, my favorite subject. I succeeded at making my parents, especially my mother, proud. My father never bragged on me like Mom and Joseph did, but in his own way he showed me, with a slight smile and a tender look, that he was proud of me too.

Shortly before I started third grade, my father asked me one Sunday how I felt about the upcoming school year. Of course we sat in Roy Rogers. I fiddled with the foil sandwich wrapper unfurled on my tray. I said I felt happy about it. A dark knowing furrowed the arch of my father's thick brows.

"Why?" he asked. Despite my success the year before, my optimism seemed to surprise him.

"Because it's a new school year!" Wasn't that obvious?

He tilted his head from side to side. "New isn't always good, Yemi. Sometimes it is, but not always. You hear me? New is not always better."

I nodded, hearing him even though I didn't want to. I wanted new to equal good. I wanted the new year to mean that what was bad—no friends—would be good, and what was already good—academic success—would be better. I wanted him to be wrong, but I never forgot his warning. Third grade wouldn't let me.

◆◆◆◆◆◆◆

My third-grade teacher, Mrs. Shelley, like Sister Antoinette, was middle-aged, but she acted much older. She walked slowly, had trouble remembering names, and always patted here and there on her desk in the afternoon before dismissal, as if searching for something in the dark. Ms. Hayes, the teacher's aide, had eyes and ears enough for both of them. Only, Ms. Hayes's focus rested squarely on me. If I pushed my glasses up my nose, from wherever Ms. Hayes stood in the room, she would snap, "William, stop fidgeting." If I stood up to go sharpen my pencil, Ms. Hayes would yell, "Sit down!" If a classmate addressed me and I started to utter a word in response, Ms. Hayes would shout, "William, be quiet!" Whereas Sister Antoinette had treated everyone in my second-grade class the same, Ms. Hayes made sure that I didn't belong.

By Halloween, Ms. Hayes was sending me to Principal Smith's office at least once a week. If I didn't sit statue-still, Ms. Hayes reported my lack of self-control. If I looked up from my work to turn something over in my mind, Ms. Hayes put a note in my backpack saying that I had been distracted that day. While Ms. Hayes rode me day in and day out, other kids got away with throwing spitballs, hitting each other, and occasionally nabbing an eraser from someone else's desk. Every bad thing they did was ignored. All I had to do was ask a question, volunteer an answer, or offer to help a classmate to get reprimanded.

It was around Thanksgiving. Posters of happy cartoon turkeys and yellow-haired pilgrims adorned the hallways. After recess, in loose formation with my class, I stopped to take a drink from a water fountain. Ms. Hayes declared that would be the last drink of water I'd have that week. "Seriously?" I said. Seconds later, one of my classmates kneed another classmate, a girl, in the back. The little girl yelped and stumbled forward. Ms. Hayes looked straight at me and yelled, "Look what you've done now, William!" She saw that I couldn't have done what she accused me of, but her bias overrode reality. A girl who was behind me at the water fountain spoke up for me. "He didn't do anything, Ms. Hayes! He was just getting a drink of water!" But Ms. Hayes wouldn't or couldn't hear it, and I was once again marched down to the principal's office for creating a disturbance.

Even now, decades later, making emotional sense of third grade is tough. The father in me registers it viscerally: a condensed mass of fury and outrage, like a storm system on a weather map. The memories stir up in me, an attorney and a public servant, the energy and doggedness of the advocate, the organizer, the education-policy wonk. And then there's this other piece of myself that understands my third-grade year as a kind of dystopian nightmare. I spent nine months in a hostility bubble under the surveillance of a menacing authority.

For Black children across this country, a dystopian education, under hostile surveillance, constitutes a long-standing norm, a warped reality where raising a hand to go to the bathroom is seen as a crime. The cases of little kids handcuffed and pepper sprayed in schools testifies to how far the demonization of Black children can escalate, to say nothing of the school-to-prison pipeline. For me, the worst part, especially about young kids being racially profiled in school, is that they can't be expected to understand that what's happening to them is not their fault. A kindergartner or first or second grader can't comprehend that part of why they've been restrained and body-slammed is because of the systemic strength and concentrated vigor of white supremacy through-out our society and especially in our education system. But kids do absorb white supremacy's virulent toxicity. It's a full-time struggle not to.

◆◆◆◆◆◆◆

Despite Ms. Hayes's best efforts to tear me down, I still man-aged to excel at math, my favorite subject. I took comfort in the fact that there was just a single correct answer, and even when Ms. Hayes graded our homework and tests, she couldn't take points off because my answers were right, end of story. I enjoyed memorizing my times tables; I liked checking over my work; I even looked forward to the tests on Fridays. I remem-ber a particular Friday clearly. We had worked on multiplica-tion into the tens that entire week. Ms. Hayes handed out the test. As soon as the paper hit my desk I got to work. Minutes later, at the second or third problem, I felt someone's eyes on me. I shot a quick glance over my shoulder. Ms. Hayes stood near the door, surveying the class. Afraid of drawing her atten-tion, I hunched over my work, trying as best I could to shield myself, to make myself invisible.

"Pssssssst," the boy beside me said. "Pssssssst," he did it again, and I tried to ignore him. Of course his whisper and my posture drew Ms. Hayes's attention.

"I know what's going on over there!" she barked. The boy innocently looked down at his paper, pretending to work on the test. Meanwhile, I stared straight ahead as Ms. Hayes snatched the test from my desk. She held the paper up close to my face and ripped it down the middle. Another kid gasped. I was too angry to speak. "Cheaters earn zeros," Ms. Hayes de-clared. "I knew all along you weren't earning those hundreds!

Go to Principal Smith's office now," she ordered. "March!" She scribbled a note to send me with and stuffed it into my hand. I stood and kicked my chair behind me.

Bureaucratic ice hardened her words. "That behavior will get you suspended, William." She added another damning sentence to the note.

I pointed at the boy. "He's the one that tried to cheat! I didn't do anything except for the test!"

"Oh, you cheated all right. I saw it with my own eyes. Then you kicked that chair when you got caught. To top it all off, you're talking back to me. You're just having a banner day, aren't you, William?" She scribbled furiously on the note and handed it to me with a triumphant smile. "Principal Smith will know exactly what to do with you."

◆◆◆◆◆◆◆

There's no counting how many times I asked Joseph the same question over the course of that school year. "Is she really treating me this way because I'm Black? Just because I'm Black?!" Unable to sugarcoat it, he'd answer with a matter-of-fact "Yes." Still of the old-school mindset that racism could be softened by compliance and an onslaught of "Yes, Ma'ams," he kept encouraging me to be polite to Ms. Hayes, not to protest even when I knew she was wrong, and to volunteer for classroom chores. Be politer, add more thank-yous, don't talk back.

I did try to be polite, but I couldn't bring myself to swallow her lies about me, much less offer to be helpful to her. Mom advocated for me to be moved to another class. There was no room, she was told, except for me to improve my disruptive behavior. Mom encouraged me to hold my ground. "You're the smartest little boy," she said. "Everyone knows it. You just have to be sure to remember it, too." Armored by my mother's confidence, I focused on making it to the end of the school year.

Springtime announced it had nearly arrived. Despite not really having friends after almost two years at Lourdes, I still loved recess. One day, a blond boy with a bowl cut from the other third-grade class joined my section's game of tag.

"Why is your hair like that?" he asked.

I had an attitude. "Like what?"

"Dirty!" He reached his hand toward my head, my hair. I swatted him away so hard my hand stung from the blow, and my body tensed, expecting him to hit me back. Instead, he caterwauled to the whole playground, "William hit me!"

A playground aide hurried over. "Are you okay?" she asked the blond boy. Stunned silent now, his face reddened. Where I had hit him on his forearm matched his cheeks. The aide knelt and held the child's arm. "You'll be alright, honey, you will," she comforted him, sweetly chucking his chin.

"I will?" The boy sought further affirmation, pitifully.

"Of course, honey," she said. Then she dealt with me.

"Why did you hit Bobby?"

Shame, humiliation, and confusion froze my tongue.

"You don't have anything to say for yourself, do you?"

What could I have said? I wasn't going to lie and say that I hadn't hit him. But I also couldn't explain why I had. A kid, and a demoralized upset one at that, I didn't have the where-withal to explain what required no justification: My hair is coily, not dirty, and it's not okay to touch my hair. I'm a Black child, not an exhibit at a petting zoo. For the rest of recess, I sat in detention where I put my head down, pounded on the desk, and cried. That night, at home, I stared in the bathroom mirror touching my uneven afro.

"You okay in there?" Mom said through the door.

"Uh-huh."

I must not have been too convincing, because Mom opened the door and stood in the frame. Her eyes were watery. "I got a call at work about a detention. What happened?"

Dread numbed my fingertips. But telling her what happened was the only chance I had of feeling better. "A boy called my hair dirty." My voice broke. "He tried to touch my hair. I hit him."

"Oh, William." She stroked my head and planted kisses all over my head. "Your hair is beautiful. So, so beautiful," she said. "Why do you think I set mine with those pink sponge rollers you're always laughing about?"

"I don't know."

"To make it curly," she said. "Like yours."

Up until then my mother had cut my hair with an old pair of clippers in the tub, a carryover practice from her time with my father. From that day forward, she never did that again. That night, Mom told Joseph that it was time for me to get a real haircut. The following Saturday, Joseph ferried me to City Cuts in downtown Silver Spring where I met Dexter, my barber for the next two decades. On the way there, Joseph informed me that men talk like men at barbershops whether kids are there or not. "You're old enough to get a professional haircut and old enough to know never to repeat what you hear."

Unsure of what Joseph was talking about, I was also certain he was right.

We arrived at the shop. Joseph pointed to a young guy brushing the nape of a customer's neck. "That's Dexter," Joseph said. "He's going to give you your first cut."

"Soon as I'm finished here," Dexter called. "Hey, Joseph."

"Hey, Dex," Joseph said. "Take care of my son, alright."

Dexter nodded. "Sure thing."

A few minutes later, Dexter waved me over to his chair, grabbed a fresh cape, and shook it out before fastening it around my neck. "Any particular requests?"

"Make me look good," I answered.

Dexter laughed. "Somebody here got his eye on the prize."

At first, I watched Dexter working on me in the mirror, his eyes focused on my hair and his tool, not his hands. His attentiveness and expertise immediately obvious, I stopped watching him and just started soaking up the atmosphere of the shop. Men, young and old, exchanged jibes. The laughter never dropped to a minor key. A radio played, so did a television, and the cacophony of the voices hemmed in on all sides by the buzz of the clippers made the space reverberate and feel big as a stadium. The presence and ubiquity of Black men in this protected space speaking without inhibition, when they felt like it, filled me with awe. It also put me at ease. Everyone at the barbershop looked different, but everyone also looked like me. They had my hair. Coily, not dirty. The barbershop was the opposite of school. I fit in and liked how it felt.

"I'm done." Dexter handed me a mirror and swiveled my chair so I could appreciate my fresh cut from all sides. Then I examined it again. "Look good?" Dexter asked.

"It looks great," I said. My hair was shorter, but I felt seven feet tall.

◆◆◆◆◆◆

At the end of the school year, my mother withdrew me from Lourdes. By that time, she had already started visiting other Catholic schools in the area. I refused to go with her.

"I want to try public school," I pleaded. "I've been to two Catholic ones. I've never been to a public one. Please, Mom. Maybe it will be better."

"How do you mean, better?"

"I might not hate it," I said.

Joseph asked, "Do you hate school now?" The son of a schoolteacher he worshiped, his voice ached.

"Yes," I answered. "I do."

"That's reason enough, Kathy. Let him try public school. He's too smart to be hating anything, let alone school. We've been told this school is the best. But they keep telling our boy that he ain't shit. We can't let this continue. We can't."

Mom nodded sorrowfully. What she assumed would be best for me turned out to be a mistake. "I'm sorry, William. I thought Lourdes would be good for you, that it would give you opportunities, and prepare you for the world. In the worst way, I turned out to be right."

"Does that mean I can go to public school?" I looked to Mom, then Joseph, and then back to Mom.

"Yes. It does." She took a deep breath. "We tried one way. Let's try another."

❖❖❖❖❖❖❖

It was great to be one Black kid among many at Oak View, but what really surprised me was the low expectations of us as a group. Math with Mr. Williams was my only challenging class because it was actually on grade level. In language arts, we started the year covering word families and vowels. The vocabulary words were as basic as *cat* and *dog*. In social studies, we talked about holidays and how to use community resources like the library. I constantly volunteered to read out loud because so few of my peers could do so fluently.

Around this time, on our Sunday visits, my father started asking me to look through *The Washington Post* and tell him what I found interesting. It was a great break from the

customary staring and silence, and I became quite the moti-
vated reader, scouring the sports section especially. Michael
Jordan, Hakeem Olajuwon, and Tim Hardaway were my favorites. Their supreme skill, their brilliance, their stardom left
me awestruck. I wanted to learn how to play in part because I
wanted to learn how to be Black, admired, and respected, all
at the same time. What jumped out at me reading the paper is
that most of the prestige those men earned came down to
numbers: the stats they put up and the salaries they took
home. As for my father, he hadn't quite given up on another
form of competition.

He squeezed some lemon in his tea. "How is Joseph?"

Anxious to change the subject, I answered, "He's fine, but
I have a teacher at school—"

My father laughed a little, cutting me off. "I would hope so."

"Do you even know I started a new school?" I backtracked,
annoyed.

"Of course I do," my father answered, and the softness in
his voice surprised me. I had never really talked to him about
Lourdes and I'm not sure Mom shared much with him either.
My father contributed what he could to my tuition. The fact
that he couldn't contribute much, I realize now, must have
embarrassed him, making it hard for him to hear about what
he couldn't pay for. Besides, the emotional price I paid at
Lourdes was so high I couldn't bring myself to discuss it with
him. The subject of Mr. Williams, on the other hand, was a
different story. It was one I badly wanted to share.

I'm not sure I had ever seen Joseph in a tie, aside from the
day he and Mom got married. I don't think I had ever seen my
father in one, either. The men I saw dressed to the nines, I
observed in one of two places: on Sunday mornings around
the neighborhood going to church, and on billboards advertis-
ing alcohol and cigarettes. A Black man in a suit represented

the dichotomy of virtue and vice, Sunday morning versus Saturday night. But Mr. Williams wasn't dressed up for the weekend. Dressed for work, ready for work, this suit and tie was his Monday through Friday uniform.

"My math teacher is Black!" I announced. The mere fact of this excited me. "His name is Mr. Williams. He wears a tie every day!"

My father's eyes lit up. "Every day?"

"Yes, every single solitary day! One day it is one color, the next it is another!"

Taking a moment to comb his memory, my father asked thoughtfully, "Is Mr. Williams your first Black teacher, Yemi?"

"Yes, he is."

My father's brow knitted. He looked as if he had just discovered what he'd been looking for for a long time. "At home, Yemi, all my teachers were Black, Nigerian like me."

"All of them?!" My disbelief turned my father's eyes sadder. "When I came to the States, I thought mostly of what I could give my family here that I couldn't at home. I'm only starting to understand what we lost, Yemi. What we lost . . ." His voice trailed off.

In that moment I realized that my father was speaking of something deep and lasting.

Later that week after about the hundredth time I mentioned that Mr. Williams wore a tie every day, Joseph commented, "You know who Mr. Williams reminds me of?"

"Who?" I asked, intrigued.

"My mom's colleagues, when she was a teacher in DC, back in the day. Those men served with pride. It sounds like Mr. Williams does, too."

Decades earlier, at Lucretia Mott Elementary in northeast Washington, DC, where Joseph's mother had spent her teaching career and where Joseph had attended lectures on the responsibility Black children have to their community, having a Black man for a teacher was not unusual. Years later, in the same community where Black male teachers had since disappeared, Mr. Williams seemed almost unreal because the presence of someone like him in a school building was so rare. Joseph's paeans to respectability politics never sat right with me, but the presence of Mr. Williams helped me to understand why respectability politics has legs at all. Mr. Williams mentored all his students by showing us that being *respectable* has as much to do with how you treat other people as it does with how you carry yourself. The virtue of respectability politics is not found in appearing respectable to outsiders. Rather it's about showing respect and care to one's own community.

Joseph gave me this framework for understanding through his stories. Mr. Williams was the one who showed me that the quality of Black life Joseph lamented as lost was not a myth. It was real in Mr. Williams, and Mr. Williams made it real for me.

◆◆◆◆◆◆◆

In math class, I raised my hand constantly without fear of being chastised. Mr. Williams called on me an average of twice during a lesson and he often encouraged the other kids by saying things like, "William, let so-and-so have a try! There's only one right answer, but the best part of math is that we can all find it!" That was true, but I still vigilantly guarded my work, hunched over my worksheets, making a barrier around my paper with my forearms. One day Mr. Williams called me on it.

"Son," he said. "With all the smarts you have, I think you could stand to share some with the other kids."

"You mean cheat?" I countered, incredulous.

Mr. Williams shook his head, kindness glinting in his dark eyes. "No, son, I'm not talking about cheating. I'm talking about helping. Come on now, you two." He touched the desk of the boy beside me. "Let's move your desks together. Everyone, please move your desk beside a partner. We're going to do these practice problems in pairs, together, from now on." Furniture screeched across the floor, and the chatter of the kids had an upbeat sound. I was one of the doubters.

"Really?" I inquired, looking up at my idol. "We're going to help each other?"

"Yes." He smiled. "That's exactly what we're going to do."

For the rest of the year, we did at least one problem with a partner during practice sets. When it took some students longer than others to finish, Mr. Williams would say something that I've since learned is attributed to Confucius: "It doesn't matter how slow you go as long as you don't stop."

Everyone supported those classmates who were struggling by chanting for ten or fifteen seconds, "Don't stop! Don't stop!" The kids who needed more time buckled down, buoyed by everyone's support. "Nice work," Mr. Williams announced to the class before correcting a single problem. The team spirit he witnessed mattered to him as much as the outcome.

We had just started a unit on fractions, and a girl raised her hand. "I got a question," she said. Two thick braids ran down each side of her head like perfect ebony latticework.

"You *have* a question," Mr. Williams gently corrected her. He may have taught math, but he offered us grammar instruction and elocution on the side.

"I have a question," she repeated back to him. Mr. Williams nodded for her to go ahead. The girl started again. "When me and my sister—"

"'Me and my sister'?" Mr. Williams repeated back to her, his eyes wide.

Unsure of what she had said or didn't say, how she had said it, or how she was actually supposed to say it, the girl started to shrink. Mr. Williams went to the girl's desk in the middle of the room. He knelt at it so that his eyes were on level with hers. Another teacher may have intimidated the little girl with proximity. Instead Mr. Williams put her at ease with his closeness.

"We're not going to tackle subject and object pronouns today. This is math after all," he said. "But there's a simple rule and I'm going to share it with you: At the beginning of a sentence you say, 'My sister and I.' At the end of a sentence, you say, 'My sister and me.' Got it?"

"Yes," she answered. The little girl's comprehension seeded within her confidence and calm, the qualities that Mr. Williams couldn't help but instill.

"Can you try again, please?" Mr. Williams asked.

The little girl swallowed. "When my sister and I were doing mixed-number fractions . . ."

"Yes!" Mr. Williams said.

The girl smiled but then said, "I can't remember!" Now everyone did laugh, including Mr. Williams, but without judgment. I remembered that I had a question and since it didn't have anything to do with math I felt this was my chance to raise my hand.

"Yes, William."

"Mr. Williams, why do you wear a tie every day?" The class broke out in a chorus of "Yes, why do you?" and "I can't believe William said that!" Mr. Williams went to the front of the room, grabbed his gray blazer from the chair, and put it on. Mr. Williams emanated seriousness and a palpable dignity. The class grew silent, and in the hush, I felt truly seen by him. Not because Mr. Williams praised me, but because he respected me. He respected all of us.

Mr. Williams asked, "Have you ever seen footage from the Civil Rights Movement?"

"Yes," I answered. "It plays on TV around Martin Luther King Jr. Day."

"What kinds of clothes did the people wear who were marching?" Mr. Williams paused. "When they were being beaten up, blasted with fire hoses, and attacked by dogs?"

"Nice shirts with collars and ties," I answered, the black-and-white footage playing in my mind. "And the ladies all wore dresses and skirts." Suddenly, I contemplated the strangeness of getting dressed up to be harassed, attacked, and possibly killed. It was like dressing yourself for your own funeral.

"That's right. The marchers wore their Sunday best because they were holy warriors. The schools, streets, and lunch counters were their church. Protest was their prayer. Those brave people got all dressed up to do the highest good they could, with the whole nation watching. My job here is easy by comparison," he finished. "I'm just trying to set an example for all of you."

In this moment, Mr. Williams mentored his students by highlighting the sacrifice of those who had come before, while he positioned us to learn from and help one another. Role models embody a goal. Mentors help others reach a goal. Mr. Williams was a mentor. His goal was that his students learn how to lift one another up.

❖❖❖❖❖❖❖

I waited for the bus after school on bustling Wayne Avenue. It was a straight shot from Oak View to my parents' office in downtown Silver Spring. It was the end of the school year, the weather was hot, and a restlessness had started to take hold. Everyone felt it. It had become hard to sit behind our desks all day.

Someone who couldn't be bothered to carry a copy of *The Washington Post* had left it on the bench in the bus shelter. I picked it up and dove into the sports section. I especially wanted to know how the Chicago Bulls and the Golden State Warriors did the night before. A moment or two later, a force punched the paper into my face. Everything went dark and the dank smell of the paper, its taste, the ink, made me sick. What was happening? Was this an accident? A mistake? An attack? My glasses askew, I was startled, confused, and nearly lost my footing as I struggled to stand and get the paper off my face. Once I did, an unfamiliar face met mine. I was being jumped, and it regularly happened to kids alone at the wrong time in the wrong place. My routine hadn't changed, but maybe neither did that of the kid who attacked me. He found a target.

Another Black boy, probably no more than a year or two older, rammed my back into the bus shelter. I put my hands around his neck and heaved him off me. Kids from school gathered around, jeering and bumping into each other like music fans in a mosh pit. The boy rushed at me again, trying to wrench me into a headlock. I punched him in the chest and he bent over, gasping for breath.

Just as the squeaky brakes of the arriving bus put the whole scene on pause, I remembered that I needed to catch the bus. I *had to* catch the bus, which pulled in so close to the curb that I jumped back, fearful it would hit me. Then, as I sprinted toward the front doors, sheets of newsprint a crumpled mess at my feet, I was yanked backward. The kid had grabbed my backpack. I gripped my straps and threw my weight forward. The fabric ripped, but the boy had lost his grip on my pack. The bus doors wheezed open and I hurried up the stairs. As I walked down the aisle of the lurching bus, most people ignored me, though some met my eyes sympathetically. Disheveled, my glasses sideways, panting and sweaty, I stared out the window, clutching a pole beside me to keep me upright.

◆◆◆◆◆◆◆

I told Mom that my backpack got ripped while I was horsing around at the bus stop. With a gaping hole above the zipper track, the bag looked like it had been knifed. I'm not sure Mom believed me, but she didn't question me either. That backpack had nearly lasted through fourth grade. Next year, I would get a new one.

The following day, I lingered in the bathroom before leaving the building for the bus stop. Though I would fight if someone provoked me, I tried my best to avoid any conflict. Waiting out the crowd was my best and only strategy. This strategy broke my way. When I finally left the bathroom, I saw Mr. Williams down the hallway in his suit and tie laughing it up with one of the janitors.

"Man," Mr. Williams said a bit scoldingly, "you're throwing away a lot of dough on that bet . . ." The janitor saw me first and nodded in my direction.

"William," Mr. Williams said, uncertainty and concern mixing in his baritone. "You're around here pretty late!" The janitor politely stepped away. Another Black man, he and Mr. Williams were clearly friends.

Mr. Williams stood less than arm's length away now, studying my face. Rather than look at him, I stared at his navy tie adorned with tiny gray polka dots. I might not have been able to tell Mr. Williams what happened directly, but I could tell his tie. It all poured out, between tears and husky breathlessness. I described the fight at the bus stop. I explained how I didn't have Cross Colours outfits or Nikes to help me fit in. Or any friends at this school or my last one. Mr. Williams listened attentively. When I finished, he said, "I'd like to teach you something, William." I could tell from the solemnity of his expression that it was going to be important.

"What's that, Mr. Williams?"

"I want to teach you to tie a half-Windsor knot." He loosened his tie by first grabbing the knot and then he put his thumb under the part of the tie that resided beneath his shirt collar. He pulled the other side of the tie and the knot vanished. He walked behind me, popped the collar on my red polo shirt, and draped the tie underneath it. "My dad showed me how to do this from behind while I sat down. Standing up will have to do now."

He instructed me to let the thicker end hang longer than the skinny one, crossed over the thick part, and then doubled it back before flipping it to the other side. Holding the knot together at the base of my neck with his fingertips he put the thick part of the tie through the neck loop. Then he grabbed the point of the thick end and tucked it into the knot. Pulling it all the way through, he cinched up the knot by tugging on the skinny end. "We're done," he said. "Want to go in the bathroom and give it a look?" I patted the neat triangle at the base of my neck. It had the power of a talisman, a charm.

"I'll bring it back tomorrow," I told him.

"No, no," he said. "It's all yours."

"You mean your tie? It's mine?"

"Yes, consider it an end-of-school-year gift."

I ran my hand over the silky fabric. "How can I thank you?"

"Just be the best fifth grader you can be next year, okay?"

Pride coursed through me as I smiled and nodded. It was like I had won first place in a contest. Only my ribbon was a tie that my very own hero bestowed upon me.

"See you tomorrow," Mr. Williams said. And those are the last words I remember him saying to me.

The following summer Mom and Joseph decided to withdraw me from our neighborhood school. The test scores were below standard and I hadn't made a single friend. But at Oak View, I had my first and only Black male teacher. I graduated from high school without ever having another for an academic subject again.

◆◆◆◆◆◆◆

The research on race and education is clear. One Black teacher in third, fourth, or fifth grade can radically shift the prospects of Black children, especially impoverished Black boys. A Johns Hopkins study showed that one Black teacher in elementary school decreases dropout rates nearly 40 percent while increasing interest in higher education by nearly 30 percent. Researchers call this "the race match effect" or the "role model effect." Black children perform for teachers, not grades. Black teachers also expect more from Black students and can coax better outcomes from them through instruction, care, and cultural familiarity. Because they look like their students, their students trust them, and begin to have more hope and trust in themselves and their futures as a result. The presence of a Black teacher has the power to communicate to Black children that higher education and professional success are not mere pipe dreams, but plans they can execute in their own lives. If their Black teachers succeeded at school, they can too.

While all this is true, only 7 to 8 percent of American teachers are Black, and only 2 percent are Black men. One way to close the long-standing opportunity gap between Black and white students in this country is to launch a large-scale recruitment and retention effort of Black teachers, especially Black men. This process may not solve the problem overnight, but the goal is worth striving for since the stakes are so high.

I touch those stakes every time I put on a tie. I felt those stakes when Joseph took me to buy a suit and tie for my middle school graduation. I felt them again at my high school, college, and law school graduations. When I got dressed for my first official day of work at the White House, I felt the presence of Mr. Williams. I remembered the feeling of his arms over my shoulders and how I watched his hands display for me what he had made a career of as he demonstrated how to put on a tie: showing care and imparting skills, giving of himself. It's not that ties in and of themselves are so important. I'm not sure my son who is a toddler as I write this will grow up to wear one very often, if ever. Mr. Williams considered his students, low-income Black and brown kids, important enough to get dressed up for. It's the sense that Black kids matter that Mr. Williams imparted to me. That's why I consider him one of my seven Black fathers. He gave me much more than his tie that afternoon. Mr. Williams returned to me my self-respect after it was nearly shattered at a bus stop and at mostly white Catholic schools. I never laid eyes on Mr. Williams after fourth grade or even learned his first name, but what sticks with me most is that I never got to thank him. So I'll do it now—thank you Mr. Williams, thank you.

3

JAY FLETCHER

FOR FIFTH GRADE, MY PARENTS ENROLLED ME AT ST. MI-chael's, a large brick Catholic school in downtown Silver Spring, just a few blocks from my mom and Joseph's office, Business Publishers Inc. (BPI). My new school's student body, working-class and majority-minority, stood in stark contrast to the population at Lourdes. But this was no nonracist, academics-focused promised land. The principal at St. Michael's, Sister Mary Neeson, a chain-smoking older white nun, held racist attitudes deeply rooted in church doctrine. Though academic standards were higher than at Oak View, the benchmarks at St. Michael's came in lower than those at the white private schools in the area. Still, I liked St. Michael's considerably better than my previous two schools.

The kids at St. Michael's, like me, were the children of working-class African Americans and Black and Latino immigrants who couldn't afford the "best" education for their kids. Like my parents, these families were not willing to arbitrarily cap their children's potential by sending them to neighborhood schools that the community openly designated as dead ends. So they scrimped, saved, and marshaled whatever resources they could to invest in their children's futures. No one at St. Michael's went to fancy places over the weekend, or took exotic vacations for spring break. No one wanted to touch my hair. No one thought the color of my skin rubbed off like shoe polish. For a kid who just wanted to fit in, I discovered at St. Michael's how good it felt not to stand out.

There were two kinds of kids at St. Michael's: destination kids and decision kids. Destination kids, like me, were expected to be somewhere by a certain time after school. Decision kids, on the other hand, had to decide where they were going, who they were going with, and why.

Some kids went to the parking lot across the street after school where fights were always flaring up. Other kids hung out on our playground, the concrete blacktop with a few basketball hoops, enclosed by a chain-link fence, abutting busy Wayne Avenue where the roar of bus engines was a constant backdrop. On the basketball courts, where I would have chosen to spend all my time, deep friendships developed. But I couldn't spend the hours I wanted to on the court, at least not in fifth and sixth grade, because I was a destination kid.

Research tells us that during the hours between 3:00 and 6:00 p.m., when parents or guardians are typically not home from work, many kids begin experimenting with drugs, alcohol, and crime. Either kids will have somewhere safe and constructive to go, like an after-school program, or they will be left to figure it out for themselves. For every child fortunate enough to be in a quality after-school program, three are on a wait list. But without the benefit of a formal activity, I had something that may have been better: my parents' office.

Every day after school I headed to BPI, where I spent time with three of the men I write about in this book, including Joseph. One of those men, Jay Fletcher, the first openly gay person who I ever met, showed me that being whole, and becoming whoever I wanted to be, meant learning to express my vulnerability, and to find my strength in doing so. Jay taught me that everyday life is an art, and with my thoughts and my words, I could write my own story.

We all can.

✦✦✦✦✦✦✦

BPI was founded in 1963 by a man called Leonard Eiserer. A mentor to Joseph, hiring him right out of high school, Mr. Eiserer, who also generously supported my education from ninth grade through law school, began his journalism career as an aviation reporter, observing how industries like big oil and manufacturing interacted with DC policy makers in the heyday of the postwar boom. Then one of the most important books of the twentieth century dramatically recontextualized Mr. Eiserer's life's work. *Silent Spring* by Rachel Carson turned Mr. Eiserer, who was once Carson's neighbor, into a staunch environmentalist. Mr. Eiserer opened BPI with the first-ever environmental newsletter, *Air/Water Pollution Report*, which documented manufacturing emissions, hazardous chemicals, and the effects of air and water pollution on human health. His philosophy of "the common good," originating in his environmentalism, defined the business and the office's culture. A diverse staff thrived there. With divisions covering the environment, aging, employment, human services, and economic fairness, BPI published fifty newsletters at its peak. A graphic art major in college, Mom helmed the production team while Joseph led the printshop. In the eighties and nineties, when I was growing up, the company employed roughly sixty full-time journalists and editors. One journalist, Jay Fletcher, mahogany brown, six feet two, and athletic, started at BPI in August 1989. I met him that same year when I was just six years old.

Mom and Joseph loved it that someone as "cultured" as Jay took an interest in me. One weekend, Jay might take me to an art exhibit and we'd look at the art first and people watch second. It usually bored me a little, but I also liked it because it was different, and Jay told me about things like impressionism and the Harlem Renaissance when we saw a painting from one of those movements. Another time, Jay tried to build my cardio by running me around the town's cracked blacktop tennis court. Jay, Joseph, and my mother were all long-time colleagues. Because Jay knew my parents he understood that I needed exposure to things beyond those that interested them, or that they had time for. And my parents trusted Jay with me. They were right to.

❖❖❖❖❖❖❖

Jay carried himself with a confidence at once innate and earned. He looked people in the eye because he believed they were as deserving of attention as he was himself. He treated people as equals, including me as a little kid, because he believed no one was above or beneath his station, which he filled with art, wit, and a sense of healthy competition. One of the first things I remember us doing together is playing games, everything from Risk, backgammon, and chess to gin rummy. Because he encouraged me to be openly competitive with him, I not only felt comfortable with Jay, but I felt comfortable being mouthy and confrontational with him too. Jay was my sparring partner, and I could always count on him to spar right back.

Afternoons in the office, I bounced between Mom's cubicle in the production department and Jay's on the editorial side, where he sat with other journalists in what they called "the pit." I sussed out who looked bored or between tasks and talked to that person. Of course, some of my parents' colleagues ignored me because they were busy or because they didn't like the idea of a little kid roaming around the office. But overall, the people who worked at BPI were kind, and frankly, looking back, I think I entertained a few of them when they weren't on deadline. I chatted away about episodes of *A Different World* and *The Cosby Show*. I explained things that I had learned in school. I also rattled off questions. Why was Bethesda a nicer place to go to school than Silver Spring? Why did people sometimes stare at Mom and Joseph? Why did some people live on the street? Unlike at school, I felt free at the office to ask as many questions as I liked.

One of many binary ideas that Catholic school got into my head is that people who believe in God are good and people who don't believe in God are bad. Simple, tribal, fixed, this stark code appealed to me as a third grader. It appealed to Jay, as a thirty-five-year-old man minding his business at the Xerox machine, not at all when I appeared at his side and asked, "Do you believe in God?"

Devilishly, a spark flashed in his eye. "No."

"You're going to hell." I pointed squarely at his chest. If I had known the word, I would have called him a heretic.

"Haven't you learned that it's a sin to judge?" Jay's righteousness rose to the surface and his smooth dark skin glowed with satisfaction.

I nodded hesitantly, suspicious that I had fallen into a trap. Which I had.

"Then aren't you going to hell for judging me?" Jay demonstrated dogma's main application: to make hypocrites of us all. A weird existential terror washed over me. I was going to die and go to hell for judging Jay. There was only one person who could help with any of this.

"Mom!" I cried as I bounded to her office in production. "Jay said I'm going to hell!" My mother's eyes rose from the paper she held in her hand, the steel in her expression icing out the surprise.

"He said what?"

"He said I'm going to hell," I repeated.

"Where is he?"

"The Xerox machine."

Colleagues darted their eyes at each other, as if ready to take cover. My mother was on the warpath to protect her cub, for a time anyway, and her defense made me feel blameless. All five feet of her stormed over to the copier to confront Jay.

"What did you say to my son?" She placed her hand on the machine.

"William already told you. He told the whole office."

"Why would you say such a thing to a child? Why?" Jay hadn't offended Mom's sense of religion or spirituality. He had offended her sense of decency, her propriety.

"If the boy can dish it, he can take it," he said.

Baleful, Mom spoke very slowly. "Here's my truth, Jay. Don't talk to my son that way again. Ever."

"Understood," Jay said. "Your son, your rules."

On the car ride home that night, Mom continued to fume. Joseph thought the whole thing was hilarious, while I thought I was the one who had broken a rule, not Jay.

"I shouldn't have asked him that," I said from the back seat.

"How about we try to settle this," Joseph suggested. "William, do you like game nights and going to museums and whatnot with Jay?"

"Of course I do! Otherwise I wouldn't do those things at all!" My mother sighed.

"William." Joseph paused more thoughtfully than he had with his previous questions. "Do you think Jay is a good person?"

I answered with a quick and unequivocal "Yes."

"How come?"

"He tells me the truth."

"That's what matters. That you think he's a good person because he's honest with you. Not that you believe all the same things."

"Not even about God?" I needed to make sure.

"Especially not about God."

Both of them the children of educators, Joseph and Jay talked to me like I was intelligent, a person who could reason. But unlike Joseph, Jay fed his own intellectual curiosity and mine too with walks through galleries where elegantly dressed people stood before paintings whispering observations to each other, and in nature preserves where occasionally we'd see a person or two with binoculars taking mental notes as they bird-watched, their ears attuned to the subtle, communicative dimensions of songs, arias really, that sounded like mere squawks and squeaks to me. Chatty as he was, Jay showed me the beauty of contemplative spaces, places that can guide us all to deeper regions within ourselves where there is quiet, where the horizon is distant, yet somehow touchable. Places where you could find the divinity within yourself, that feel like the best kind of church. I may have attended Catholic school, but my family attended church only on Easter Sunday, Christmas Eve, and special occasions. I understood the term "lapsed." But atheism was a stretch, and Jay was an atheist. I decided, with Joseph's nudging, that I'd have to accept his way of thinking about God. It was part of what made Jay different from everyone else in my world. His differences were why I loved being with him.

❖❖❖❖❖❖❖

The years at Lourdes, a devout Catholic school in name, left their scars. Some of them manifested as nightmares about Ms.

Hayes. In one, she sat at a Roy Rogers booth across from my father and me, staring and silent before she bared her teeth, like a rabid dog. In the other nightmare that I can recall, I rode in the back seat of the car while my mother drove. Randomly, I glanced out the side window and when I looked forward again, my mother had disappeared. Ms. Hayes had replaced her in the driver's seat. Without speaking, she drove, thrusting the car forward as I struggled to move. I cried out for help, for my freedom, while Ms. Hayes continued to face forward, saying nothing. In fact, that was the worst part of the nightmare: her silence. By refusing to acknowledge me, it was like she had finally made me invisible once and for all. And what had she done with my mother?

At Oak View, Mr. Williams's mere presence and steadfast encouragement helped address some of this trauma, but he couldn't heal it completely. One Monday afternoon, on my way to the BPI office, I stumbled on a potent coping mechanism: food.

The previous Sunday my father had given me a few dollar bills. After school Monday, when I pulled my bus pass out of my pocket, I rediscovered the cash. In downtown Silver Spring, off Pershing Drive, a few doors down from BPI, there was a McDonald's. Because I didn't have enough money for the large combo, I ordered the double cheeseburger meal with a medium Sprite and fries for $3.14 with tax. I walked to the back of BPI and checked in with Mom, who grabbed a couple of fries to snack on at her desk, then I went into the empty conference room. As I unwrapped the food at the long Formica table and began eating, I realized how hungry I had been all day, how ravenous I always was.

On Sundays with Dad in Roy Rogers, I ate a three-piece fried chicken meal with large fries and a soda. When he dropped me off at home, I ate dinner with Mom and Joseph because I was still hungry. After I finished my McDonald's in the conference room that first time, a sense of well-being, of having enough and being enough, washed over me. I actually wasn't hungry anymore. The meal satiated me. Rather than drain me like so much of school did, the meal made me feel full, complete.

Typically, at some point in the afternoon, I'd roll up to Jay's cubicle sipping Sprite, or scraping the bottom of a carton of fries, fat crystals of salt glittering on my greasy fingertips. Jay would swivel his chair around, look at me, then swivel back to his desk, where he opened the top drawer and pulled out a short stack of brown paper napkins. I accepted them, finished chewing, and wiped my hands.

"Another round at the Double Cheeseburger Open I see."

This was Jay's way of poking fun at me over my daily McDonald's pilgrimage. The irony of referring to my eating habits as an athletic event most certainly was not lost on me.

The look of Jay's sculpted arms in his fitted sweaters and shirts always reminded me of how ripped Superman still looked even while wearing his Clark Kent disguise. Jay's clothes weren't particularly expensive, but they were always neat, well-tailored, and color coordinated. More than his clothes, Jay's style made him look good, and part of that style was that he ate right and exercised. I wore my school uniform—khaki slacks and a white oxford shirt—to the office. Outside of school, high-water jeans; funny, bulky sweaters; and no-name sneakers were my standard outfit. In either getup, my body felt as bulky as my clothes were conspicuous. Jay seemed to notice more how I felt in my clothes than what I was actually wearing.

"Hello, William," Jay invariably said with equal parts affection and puckishness.

"What are you doing?" I asked. He had a notebook scrawled

with notes to his left and two pads of Post-its, one yellow and one orange, to his right. He scribbled something on a Post-it and then stuck it to a page of his notebook.

Quickly, spritely, he answered, "Being a journalist."

"What does a journalist do?"

"Organize the facts, which is what I'm doing now. Report stories."

"Aren't stories made up?"

"Not the ones I write."

"How come?"

"Don't ask 'How come?'" Jay pretended to speak in my voice, shrugging his shoulders while he spoke and tilting his head awkwardly. Was he mocking me? Yes. Did the ribbing mean we were friends? Yes, again. "Ask *why* instead, William. *Why* is succinct. *How come* is sloppy."

I took a beat. "What's 'succinct' mean?"

"Look it up." Jay swiveled his chair back toward his desk. "You know where the dictionaries are." I went to the conference room where a lot of the office ate their lunch and where I could still smell the remnants of my cheeseburger. I spotted a dictionary in there on the shelf, pulled it down, and flipped through its hymnal-like pages.

◆◆◆◆◆◆

A week or two later, Jay took me for a Saturday bike ride on the nature trail at Long Branch Local Park. There were scrawny white-tailed deer, squirrels, and clouds of minuscule bugs that got in my mouth. Everything seemed minute except for me and the trees. I'd had another growth spurt and overnight my legs were too long for my twin bed and hanging off the bike pedals, my size-eleven feet looking bigger than they normally did. Suddenly, I felt bigger beside Jay than I normally did, and

Jay was over six feet. After about a two-mile ride, we took a break, and then walked our bikes a bit before starting up again. I was breathing heavily.

"Stop inhaling those cheeseburgers every day and you might be able to exhale better," Jay said.

"Why are you so mean?" I said. "It's because you think I'm fat, don't you? I'm not talking about the slang word p-h-a-t." I spelled it. "I'm talking about f-a-t." I spelled that too.

Jay's mouth tightened into an expression of contrition blended with pity I had never seen him wear before.

"Why do you eat McDonald's every day?" he asked.

"What's wrong with that?" My hackles rose.

"I think you're hungry for something."

"That's why I eat McDonald's! I'm hungry! Duh!"

"You're defensive," Jay diagnosed. "And that word, 'duh,' it's got to go."

We were standing in the middle of the woods, trees rising all around us. The ride had made me thirsty, hungry, insatiable. I wanted a bite of a cheeseburger. I could taste it.

"Salty, fat-laden food is not going to stop your feelings from eating you, William," Jay spoke to me evenly, almost placidly. "Notice what you're thinking about, if you're thinking about anything at all, when you register that you're hungry. Notice what you're thinking about the moment before you take your first bite. Consider talking about those feelings, those thoughts, to your parents, to me. It could help."

"I'm talking to you right now. What good is it doing? I'm hungry and you're giving me grief!"

"Let's head back to my house. I'll make you something to eat," Jay said matter-of-factly.

"What are you going to make? Something nasty?" I sneered.

Jay shook his head at my hardheadedness. "No, something healthy."

❖❖❖❖❖❖❖

As Jay started to prep the meal, placing a cutting board on the counter and peeling garlic, I went over to the kitchen phone and called my mother. I asked Mom to come pick me up.

"You sure you don't want to stay for dinner?" Mom asked.

"No, just come get me. It smells like garlic here and I don't like it." When I hung up, Jay had placed a contraption on the countertop. A pot with dials and a thermometer, it reminded me of a device the Ghostbusters used to capture ghosts.

"It's a steamer and rice cooker," he said. "I'm steaming spinach tonight."

"Sounds great but I'm going outside to wait for my mother."

"Tell her I said hello."

❖❖❖❖❖❖❖

My mother started packing apple slices with my bologna sandwich for lunch at school, and she roasted vegetables as sides for dinner at home. I did my best to avoid them. But when she fried chicken and pork chops and baked roast beef, Joseph's favorites, I inhaled those meals, as I did her perfectly moist chocolate chip cookies. But as Mom watched me devour a near-dozen of them, I could see from her expression that what I ate worried her.

She made an appointment with my pediatrician, Dr. Johnson, a kind Black woman with a pleasant, open face. Dr. Johnson greeted us cheerfully in the brightness of the exam room. Fitted and starched, her white physician's coat exuded competence, while the silk blouse she wore beneath it conveyed tenderness.

Dr. Johnson exchanged pleasantries with my mother and me, as she fitted my arm with the blood-pressure cuff. She squeezed the black plastic bulb and the cuff gripped, tightened, and released. At 132/80, my blood pressure fell into the borderline high range. At 135 pounds, even given my height, I was undeniably overweight. A few days later her office called to say that at 241, my cholesterol level was way too high for anyone, let alone a kid. My overeating and fast-food habit had put me on the fast track for type 2 diabetes. The prescription was clear: fruits, vegetables, and exercise. No more fatty foods high in sugar and sodium. No more foods that made me feel artificially full. Right away, Mom cut off my McDonald's allowance. My father and I continued to meet at Roy Rogers, only we didn't hang out and eat in our booth anymore. Instead, we walked around Silver Spring. Everyone had gotten the message.

Brattily, I lamented, "Other people can eat whatever they want. Why can't I?"

"You're an American, Yemi," my father said. "Americans cannot eat whatever they want because they have a tendency to eat everything."

A bitter taste pooled in my mouth. "Why did you even come to this country?"

My father cast his eyes downward. "I guess I wanted a little bit of everything too."

❖ ❖ ❖ ❖ ❖ ❖ ❖

Jay insisted that we visit different green spaces when we got together now. At Olney Manor Recreational Park, he gave me tennis lessons that I bombed at, unable to get the hang of manipulating my grip on the racket or hitting a decent serve. Unlike basketball, tennis was an individual sport and there was nowhere to hide. It frustrated me that I wasn't good at it, but in a way that made me want to try harder. We'd bike or walk through the woods afterward, which was fine, but not my favorite thing to do. Without knowing for certain, I was sure that Mom and Joseph had shared with Jay my poor health report. But I knew that I could change, that I *would* change, and my health would improve. I had gone from just thinking about playing basketball and reading the sports section to actually playing the game and sweating. At my urging, my parents had signed me up for the Catholic Youth Organization (CYO) team at St. Michael's. Though I remained a poor shooter and a clumsy dribbler, I worked hard and every day I moved better and felt better too.

"I miss having McDonald's," I admitted to Jay on one of our walks after tennis, "but I like that I don't *need it* every day anymore."

"William, really?" Jay seemed genuinely surprised, not at my sentiment, but that I had expressed it at all.

"Yes."

"Tell me something else you sincerely mean." Jay opened the door wide on my emotional life, leaving me flummoxed. Jay let me soak in my own uncertainty for a few moments as we walked. "Ponderous silence is better than defensive noise, William. Congratulations, you're growing up."

On one level, Jay might as well have been sharing with me the secrets of quantum physics or the nuances of seventeenth-century Arabic poetry. On another, I understood him perfectly. Sometimes my responses were rapid-fire. Other times I was lost and had no idea what to say. Now, at Jay's prompting, I was beginning to observe my thoughts and how they dictated my actions before I said a word or took a bite. This meant I spent more time listening to others, and observing my own thoughts, and less time talking and eating. Months had passed since Jay asked me why I was so hungry. I finally knew. My McDonald's habit started while I attended Oak View. The kids there had grown up together; many of them were friends in their neighborhoods. Every day, I left school feeling like an outsider. Every day, I headed directly to McDonald's the minute the dismissal bell rang.

"I wanted a friend!" I blurted. "I was hungry for a friend! School has been so hard." The tears started. "I needed a friend to make it easier, something to make it easier." I broke into full-blown sobs. We stopped walking and Jay pulled me into his side, holding me, keeping me upright.

"It's okay, William. It is. If you let the words out, you won't need to stuff all the feelings down with food. The last thing you want to do is stuff the feelings down. They could kill you. They almost killed me."

Jay's revelation stopped my tears cold. "What almost killed you?" I asked, astonished that anything, anyone, had ever menaced him.

Jay sighed, took a moment, and glanced up at the sky before meeting my gaze again. "My parents and my brother tried to make my life a living hell by constantly telling me to shut up and change. I didn't shut up because I believed in myself. I didn't change because I liked myself, and I still do. William, believe it or not I adore you and there is nothing more I want for you in this world than for you to love yourself for everything you are and everything you will be.

"Everything is not something you find anywhere but inside yourself," Jay said, and I immediately remembered the comment my father had made about Americans eating everything, about our insatiability. "You claim everything that counts when you're a friend to yourself, William," Jay continued. "A friend to yourself. If there's anything a Black man needs, it's himself as his own damn friend."

Jay brought me in closer, tighter, and the alchemy of his words, their truth, swung wide open that door to finding myself and liking myself. The question sounded so silly in my head, I almost didn't ask it, but it flew out from that place in me that Jay had unlatched: "How did you become your own friend? How did you do it?"

"I didn't have a choice," he said. "There was no one else like me, and no one else willing to grapple alongside me with how I was different, so I faced it alone and found that I alone had to accept myself. I alone had that power. No one else. I did."

All at once it tracked that Jay never had girlfriends, talked about dating, or ever brought a significant other to office parties. Pictures of family, friends, and spouses decorated everyone's cubicles at BPI, except for Jay's. He had said that his family had refused to accept him. Viscerally, I understood why. Jay was gay. His sexuality had set him apart, and in that isolation he had pieced himself together with emotional and psychological resources that he had unearthed. Jay modeled for me a vision of masculinity that was burnished in the fire of homophobia, and then vitalized and cemented by queerness, not undermined or compromised by it. Jay fortified himself by tending his difference with care and understanding, not annihilating it out of fear and mistrust. In recognizing how Jay and I were different, I found I wanted to be strong and clever just like Jay. Self-acceptance liberated Jay's thoughts from the chains of self-hatred. By defining his thoughts, Jay defined his life.

Jay was the strongest man I knew.

◆◆◆◆◆◆

Early one Saturday morning, my mother came into my room and pulled open the blinds. Annoyed, I shifted under the covers. My mother responded by pulling the blanket off me. It was Saturday and I slept in on Saturdays.

"What?" I said, still flat out in bed, cold without my blanket.

Mom ordered me up cheerfully, ignoring my mood. "You have to get dressed for the train. You're going to New York City today to see a play!"

"I am?" I sat up.

"Yes," Mom half sang. "Jay is taking you! He wanted it to be a surprise. Come on, now! You have to make the train!"

I jumped out of bed, and out of habit started to straighten the sheets. "I'll make your bed today," Mom said. "Go on, get ready!"

"What should I wear?"

"Something nice," she answered. "Decide in the shower."

I wore an ugly Cliff Huxtable sweater I got for Christmas and a pair of my uniform khakis. Joseph drove me to the station where Jay stood waiting for me. As I got out of the car, Joseph tooted the horn at Jay and drove off.

"How long have you been cooking this up?" I asked.

"Since I read *Seven Guitars* was opening on Broadway."

"*Seven Guitars*?"

"That's the name of the matinee we're going to see. I'll tell you all about it on the train."

And so Jay did. He explained that a playwright named August Wilson was writing a series of plays about the Black experience in America called the Century Cycle. Each of the works was set in Pittsburgh, where Wilson grew up, but at different points in time over the course of the twentieth century. My idea of the "Black experience" mainly consisted of black-and-white clips of dignified protesters confronting dogs, hoses, and policemen in the street, with podium footage of Martin Luther King Jr. spliced in, against a soundtrack of Joseph's stories about the good old days. As I listened to Jay from my window seat, I realized that I actually had no idea what the phrase *Black experience* meant.

"What is the Black experience?" I asked.

Jay laughed a heartier laugh than I had ever heard from him. "Chile, the Black experience clears up the confusion of our country's history. We built this country, and us Black folks are the ones who have most successfully agitated for it to be an authentic democracy. We might not own this land, but at least we now own ourselves. That's what the art we're going to see today testifies to. That people can always own outright at least one item of great value. Themselves." Jay paused. "Wait a second, William."

"I have to wait more than a second. We're stuck on this train together, remember."

"Please." Jay rolled his eyes. "You like basketball, right?"

"Yes, and . . ."

"Why?"

I had a thousand answers and no answer at all to that question. I loved basketball because it showcased greatness. And because it was competitive. And because I wanted to get better at something that had an audience. I loved basketball because I also wanted to improve at something for my own sake. Because it provided a platform for me to be and reflect everything I had learned. Basketball made me feel full.

"I just do," I answered.

"It's more than that," Jay said. "There's something about yourself that you can show through basketball that deserves to be seen." Jay again paused, halted by his own epiphany. "That's a way to define the Black experience that I've never thought of before. As something that deserves to be seen."

"I think I'm getting it now."

◆ ◆ ◆ ◆ ◆ ◆

I had never been anywhere like the Walter Kerr Theatre. Drenched in soft golden light, the theater's interior looked as if it had been removed from a storybook and plopped down smack in the middle of New York City. The red velvet seats and the great claret curtain, the gold leaf, the ceilings, and the frescoes all had the patina of a dream. The show itself, with Viola Davis starring as Vera, was mesmerizing. With an all-Black cast—which I had never seen before and that gave me chills in a good way—this was no musical, yet August Wilson's words burst forth with so much music, so much bluesy, moving singing, that a melody I couldn't place played in my head that evening the whole way home on the train. So did a thought about Jay. He was gay. Everyone knew it. The closest he had come to telling me outright was that day in the park when he shared a little bit about how his family treated him for being different and wanted him to change.

"Are you gay?" I asked plainly.

Jay's eyes bulged slightly. He took a moment, a long one. "Yes."

"How did you accept yourself, when your family didn't?" I think the genius of the play lent me some of its courage.

Jay crossed his arms, and in that gesture I could see he wasn't holding anything back as much as holding himself and examining his own life, the moments that had threatened to break him, and those that had birthed him anew.

"The last time I was in public alone with my brother," Jay said, "he asked me if I was going to be a man or gay."

Now *my* eyes bulged, saddened by the cruelty Jay had encountered, but fascinated by and admiring of how indomitable Jay's pain had made him. "How did you respond?"

"I said to him, 'Are you going to be Black or a man?'"

"What did he say?"

"My brother was no fool. He answered, 'I'm both.' I returned the volley and said, 'I'm everything you are and more: Black, gay, a man, a person.' That's always what I will tell you,

William. Express yourself and be it all. Don't let anyone tell you who you are and what you can and can't be. Think you're something and you can make yourself everything. Think you're nothing and you will never be anything. It's your decision."

Liberated by Jay's assertion and also exhausted from the day, I leaned back and stared out the window. The Amtrak cars clattered smoothly down the tracks, metronomic and percussive. In my head, I matched a guitar melody the show's murdered protagonist, a blues singer named Floyd Barton, played to the words Jay had spoken earlier about the Black experience. Part mantra, part lullaby, I fell asleep on the train repeating to myself: *The Black experience deserves to be seen / Yes, it does / Yes, it does / The Black experience deserves to be seen / Yes, it does / Yes, it does.*

More than anything, I was grateful that I got to see Jay, for everything that he was, everything that he had made of himself, and everything he showed me I could be.

4

WAYNE HOLMES

THE LATE NINETIES WERE A PROSPEROUS TIME FOR MANY Americans. While Biggie and P. Diddy famously rapped about "Mo Money Mo Problems," for regular working-class people like my family, increased financial stability meant opportunity and solutions. For years, we'd lived in the modest duplex on Eleventh Avenue in Long Branch with Joseph's family, and before that in an apartment on Quebec Terrace around the corner, where gunshots rang out regularly. After years of sacrifice, Mom and Joseph saved enough for a down payment on a small single-family home in a friendly middle-class neighborhood. My family went from renting in the working-class sections of Montgomery County to being homeowners in a community where Black folks had truly *arrived*. The shift was dramatic. For the first time in my young life, I stopped struggling and started thriving. There were a lot of kids around my age in the development, which had a basketball court all its own, and most of my socializing in the neighborhood, in the beginning at least, revolved around music and basketball.

Kalfani had introduced me to go-go back at St. Michael's, but I got deep into the music on my own, everyone from the Backyard Band and Rare Essence to even Chuck Brown and the Soul Searchers, the inventors of go-go in seventies-era DC. With kids from my new neighborhood, signs and spirited attitudes in tow, I participated in the distinctly DC metro area experience of jamming out at go-go shows, which are not just a concert, but a concert, dance party, and sporting event all rolled into one.

Everyone shows up at a go-go show in a crew, bearing colorful signs that rep their neighborhood in hopes of getting that coveted shout-out by band members, which will live forever on the go-go tapes distributed throughout the region. Between sets, the music never stops. Neither do the rap battles. Or the sweaty, shoulder-to-shoulder, call-and-response parties. And the dancing. The *dancing* . . .

Girls at go-gos were half the reason most of us boys showed up. But when the party ended and everyone split for home, I couldn't muster the words to speak to the girls I liked, when the sounds of the steel drums and percussion instruments stopped ringing in our ears and the silence cracked the night wide open. To speak to girls, when it was actually quiet, I needed confidence that matched how I had changed, and I couldn't always access it.

In middle school, the chubby, awkward kid in Rec Specs and high-water pants disappeared to the outside world. I played enough competitive basketball and put in enough practice to start losing weight. Contacts replaced my glasses. My grades improved and I told people to call me Will. But when I looked in the mirror I often saw ten- and eleven-year-old me waiting for the bus on Wayne Avenue.

◆◆◆◆◆◆◆

For high school, my parents enrolled me at St. John's College High School, an elite private school in the tony Chevy Chase neighborhood of DC. I attended on a partial scholarship and Mr. Eiserer, my parents' boss at BPI, contributed to my tuition through a philanthropic fund. Still, a mortgage and partial tuition stretched my family's budget. For my mother, it was worth it. She had finally obtained what she had struggled for years to secure on my behalf through education: opportunity as well as prestige.

◆ ◆ ◆ ◆ ◆ ◆ ◆

My freshman year I had a crush on Joy, the cousin of my friend Justin, who was two years ahead of me at school. Petite with discerning eyes set into a sensitive face, Joy made it hard to tell whether she was about to hug you or tell you off. An officer in the Cadet Corps, Joy looked great in her uniform, high-stepping in patent leather kitten heel pumps shined to a high gloss, her jacket cinched at the waist, and her green beret angled just so. Much is said about women being attracted to men in uniforms. I fall into a different camp, that of men attracted to women in uniforms.

One day in the fall of my freshman year, I spotted Joy all decked out in her cadet gear, sitting at a table in the back of the cafeteria with the other popular upperclassmen, a mix of football players and cool girls. I got my lunch and brought it to my usual table of ninth- and tenth-grade basketball players, but didn't sit. Jeff, who would become my team cocaptain senior year, asked, "You forget something?"

"No," I responded. "I have to do something."

Jeff gave me a quizzical look, but I was off. I walked to Joy's table where she sat between one of the football players and one of her girlfriends. "Hey, Joy," I said at standard volume, which in a noisy cafeteria amounted to a whisper. Nothing. "Hey, Joy." I turned it up a notch. Still nothing. "HEY, JOY!" I finally yelled. The entire table hit pause and shot their eyes at me. Expressions ranged from curious to confused. Joy delivered me the same look as Jeff had, but then she said, "Hey."

"I think you look really nice today," I said.

The boy next to her repeated my words in a Steve Urkel voice. I was a freshman and he was a beefy football player, but I didn't look away.

Joy elbowed him to pipe down, then turned her attention to me. "Thank you, Will." She gave me a head-to-toe glance. "You look nice, too."

Heat rose in my cheeks. I searched my mind for something more to say, landing on an awkward "Thanks."

Joy picked up where she had left off with her friends and the rest of her table took its cue from her. Voices rose and levity resumed. I had committed a cardinal sin for an athlete. I choked.

◆◆◆◆◆◆◆

Mr. and Mrs. Brooks, our next-door neighbors in Beltsville, both worked for the US Postal Service. Their daughter Kim was two years older than me. When she painted her nails on the patio in their backyard, I'd peek over the fence and say hi, participating in an ongoing tutorial about what makes the girl next door the girl next door. Kim was extremely close in proximity while being completely out of my reach.

"Hey, Will." She would quickly glance up from the nails she was painting a glossy pink. Her lashes were thick and her skin was brown and smooth.

"What's up, Kim?"

One time she answered "Jesus," the matter-of-fact way someone else might say "the sky," but she was serious. Kim was deeply into her church and her faith.

I smiled and said, "Yes, He is," because I had girls on the brain and I would have said anything to keep the conversation going.

"Come to Bible study the next time it's at my house."

"Really?" I half expected her to retract the invite, but my lack of confidence may have been why she'd asked me to join in the first place.

"Yes!" Kim replied. "You'll feel really welcome."

❖❖❖❖❖❖❖

All juniors and seniors from different high schools around the DC metro area, the girls sat around the patio table, posing questions about how to live more faithfully, glowing in their tank tops or deep V-necks, shorts or jeans skirts. I had questions swimming around my head, too, only they were not about God.

Did they have boyfriends? How did they always have so much to talk about? Always just one more thing to mention. And another, and another. It wasn't so much that everything they said impressed me. It was that they had a shared language for their feelings about their faith, which I didn't really understand. I believed in God, but it wasn't real for me like it was for them. The girls read my silence as shyness; they thought my reticence was evidence of my sincerity. In a way, it was.

One day Kim rang the doorbell.

"Hey." She handed me a brochure. "I think you should come to this."

"What is it?"

"It's a sleepaway Christian camp. I'm going and so are my friends. Think about it."

I didn't have to. I was in.

❖❖❖❖❖❖❖

Held at James Madison University in Virginia's lush Shenandoah Valley, the camp lasted only three days. All the participants were assigned to single-sex dorms on campus and each day workshops were scheduled on teen issues and the role of Christ. Unsurprisingly, I wasn't the only fourteen-year-old there to meet girls, and I quickly became the ringleader of some boys on my hall, maneuvering for us to sit with a new group of girls at every meal, and arriving at workshops just as they started so I could get as close as possible to the prettiest girl there. But by the end of the second day, something inside me began to shift.

My mother and my years in Catholic school had taught me to pray. I made confirmation and was an altar boy, but nothing at church or in my parochial education ever spoke to my heart. At the camp, the speakers were all from either Baptist or evangelical backgrounds, and when they spoke it felt like they were talking directly to me, a kid struggling to do the right thing in situations where being decent was often read as weakness.

Inside those workshops we talked about depression, anger, peer pressure, and sex. My parents' divorce and racism at school left me feeling unmoored, and not quite understanding what these feelings were. These preachers were beckoning me to anchor myself in faith, and I was just beginning to understand that I was adrift. They were naming my biggest fears and showing me how to make my way through them. With each session, I paid a little more attention, listened more deeply, heard more of what I needed, and allowed a new kind of feeling to enter me.

One workshop leader, a twentysomething white man, opened a session by asking, "How many of you live in single-parent homes?" One or two kids raised their hands. Then he asked, "How many of you want a better relationship with your mother?" Three or four kids raised their hands. Finally, he asked, "How many of you want a better relationship with your father?" I raised my hand immediately. So did every other kid in the room. It was the first time I had not felt alone with my disappointment in my father, and the strange disappointment with myself that followed from that.

On the last full day of camp, everyone attended a worship service. I sat in the middle of the auditorium in an aisle seat, and I let the music move through me. The drummer infused the band's beat with a soulful R&B rhythm. The preacher was a young, charismatic Black woman, and I had never seen anyone who looked like her leading a service before. She was preaching about having the courage to stand against what others think you should do and live a life dedicated to God. The worship leaders walked the aisles and sang, encouraging everyone to rise to their feet. At first, I didn't rise with the others, but then I felt moved, compelled by a sweeping, uplifting force. We all held hands and swayed.

It's hard to explain this, because I think most people don't talk about it, or when they do it's so "churchy" it feels inaccessible. But this moment was like nothing I'd ever felt before. The percussion of the drums syncopated with my heart. I remember standing with my eyes closed and lifting my hands, because suddenly keeping them at my sides felt too heavy. My breath shallowed and then deepened, and my mind cleared. Then, as if a faucet had been opened in both my heart and my eyes, the tears came rolling down and I was filled with an overwhelming sense of warmth and love. It felt like every weight I had been carrying was lifted as acceptance washed over me.

We don't talk to kids, and especially boys, enough about love. We leave them to figure it out from music, from magazines, on the theory that that is enough. But at that moment I got it. I felt loved and worthy of love. I've heard it said before that love is an action word. In that moment, the act of love found me.

One of the worship leaders, a tall Black man who I had never seen before and would never see again, wrapped his arms around me. I sobbed and convulsed into this stranger's chest and he held me, cradling the newborn spirit in me, as the Holy Ghost conducted its visitation. When he let me go, I murmured thanks, my face hot with tears. He nodded assuringly and moved on through the crowd, while it felt like the entire universe had just moved through me.

◆◆◆◆◆◆◆

When I got home, I talked with Mom and Joseph about what had happened. Catholicism had never reached my heart in that way, and I knew whatever had happened to me at camp was something I needed to investigate further. I asked to attend a Baptist church with Joseph's brother Steven and his wife, Andrea. They were the only churchgoing Baptists in the family, and they lived just a few miles away. My parents agreed and Uncle Steven and Aunt Andrea, the kind people they were, said they would be thrilled to have me join them on Sunday mornings. The child of a lapsed Nigerian Muslim and a devout American midwestern Catholic, I became an African American Baptist, a bona fide member of the Black church.

Aunt Andrea and Uncle Steven attended Mt. Pleasant Baptist Church on Rhode Island Avenue in northwest DC, led by Reverend Terry D. Streeter, who remains the senior pastor there until this day.

They called church "home" like many congregants do because that's where their hearts lived and where they were at peace. They referred to their fellow church members as family because of their shared communion with Christ. On Sunday mornings, I put on my tie like Mr. Williams had taught me and sat in the maroon cushioned pews, on the edge of my seat.

Aunt Andrea always had a piece of hard candy for me as the sermon started, and a little pat on the back for me when it ended, impressed, I think, by my rapt attention. A South Carolinian and a devoted educator who spent her entire twenty-eight-year career in an underserved elementary school in southeast DC, Aunt Andrea became my first church mother. Uncle Steven, a cook for the Defense Department, prepared and served food for the fellowship meal after church; he became my first church father. Because Uncle Steven cooked, we stayed for the food and socializing after service.

One afternoon, as Aunt Andrea and I cleared platters from the serving table, she asked me a question even my mother hadn't asked yet. "William, you have a girlfriend?"

I said I didn't, and I noticed that it didn't bother me to say so. Ever since Christian camp, I felt more connected to people and more connected to myself. The result was that talking to girls had become easier because, in general, I felt less distance than I had previously between myself and other people. I was enjoying girls as people, not as the imagined solutions to my needs, because I had found something more deeply connected to my soul to fill those needs. I hadn't registered or really processed any of this until Aunt Andrea asked.

In the Black church, responding to the altar is a public display of the desire to be "saved" from sin and an affirmation to enter into a personal relationship with God. In my case, I wanted to be saved from the emptiness I felt since first sitting in that Roy Rogers booth with my dad, or being bullied at Our Lady of Lourdes. I had a deeply ingrained sense of loneliness and discomfort about how I seemed in the world, and ever since that moment at James Madison, I understood that something about faith took some of that away.

A Sunday or two following my exchange with Aunt Andrea, the organist played "He Whom the Son Sets Free." My breath changed, hastening and shallowing before it deepened, the way it had back at camp. Reverend Streeter, a commanding and calming presence, repeated the common but moving refrain, "Tomorrow is not promised." Carried by my breath, love and acceptance moved through my body. I began to maneuver toward the aisle. To honor the faith moving through me, I had to proclaim it, testify. Aunt Andrea, observing all this, clasped my hand in hers and kissed it. Tears were running down her cheeks. The first grown Black woman whom I loved deeply, Aunt Andrea cared for me less like a nephew and more like a son. Moved to come to Jesus, to proclaim Him publicly as my savior, I journeyed down the aisle to the altar and got saved a second time. Aunt Andrea and Uncle Steven embraced me afterward as they offered tearful congratulations. The three of us, apart from my mom and Joseph, constituted a church family.

From that time until now, beginning with Reverend Streeter, I have benefitted from two additional spiritual mentors. Shortly after I was baptized, I became friends with a fellow high school basketball player named Sarah Jenkins who attended Riverdale Baptist. We shot hoops together, hung out at games, and I became a regular around her house with our group of high school guy and girl ball players, where I met her dad, John K. Jenkins Sr., the pastor at the First Baptist Church of Glenarden. Reverend Streeter may have been the first preacher I listened to with my heart in the pews, but Mr. Jenkins was the first pastor I got to observe as a caring, supportive father in the comfort of his home and from the pulpit. First as a friend of his daughter, and later as a member of his church, I was shown faith and grace in action by Pastor Jenkins—initially as a mentor when I was a teenager, and then as my minister and confidant when I faced challenges as a young man. My current pastor, Reverend Matthew L. Watley, who leads Kingdom Fellowship AME Church, the largest in Montgomery County, with five thousand members, is a peer mentor, a dear friend, and a fellow girl dad. He and his wife Shawna's eldest daughter, Ally, is best friends with my eldest daughter, Alia. Matthew, whom I admire as a minister, a thought leader, and a businessman, is also godfather to my son William Isaiah because above all, I admire how with a thousand things going on at once, the most important thing going on in Matthew's life is his family. This is something that Pastor Streeter, Pastor Jenkins, and Pastor Watley share. They are all present family men. I am proud to say that in my heart, I will always be a member of all three men's church families.

◆◆◆◆◆◆◆

One morning in homeroom during my junior year, a lanky, brown-skinned kid named Mark mentioned to me that a gospel choir might be starting up at school. I didn't let my excitement show or ask him any questions, though I badly wanted to. A few days later, Mark and his friend Denise, who wore her hair in a neat top bun and her uniform cardigan every day when no one else did, happened to be ahead of me in the lunch line. They were not unpopular, but they weren't trying to be popular, either. They were smart kids who did their own thing, and I respected that.

I tapped Mark on the shoulder. "So what's up with the gospel choir?"

They looked at me, at each other, and then slightly turned their backs. They needed to confer.

I put on my let's-be-adults-about-this voice. "Really, y'all?"

Mark awkwardly shifted his weight, seemingly embarrassed by his initial response. Denise looked disinterested.

"Well," said Mark, "there's a gospel choir at St. John's now." He gestured at Denise. "We started it."

I asked, "Who's the faculty advisor?"

"Coach Holmes." Mark smiled broadly and the mere mention of the coach's name engaged Denise.

"Our group is open," she said proudly, her top bun a pastry-like swirl. "But you should still go talk to him about it."

"I will."

◆◆◆◆◆◆◆

Whether you played football or not, and Mark and Denise were about as far from football players as you could get, everyone referred to Coach Holmes as, well, Coach Holmes or just Coach. The better the coach, the more targeted and personalized the training—the more general the moniker. I think this is because a tacit understanding emerges in communities: that the best coach isn't just any coach, but *the coach*. The best coaches are good at their jobs not because they've cracked an athletic code but because they use that knowledge to enhance the lives of their protégés, athletes, and students in ways that have nothing to do with sports. In this regard, Wayne Holmes was in a league all his own.

Six feet six and well over three hundred pounds, Coach took what he learned from football and used it not just to coach a sport, or a choir, but to shepherd an inclusive community into existence. He did so with an open-door policy. If Coach Holmes was in his classroom, the door was open. If it was before school, after school, or he was proctoring a study hall, gospel music played.

Of course Coach Holmes was the choir's faculty advisor. A St. John's alum, he was also a local legend.

In 1989, Coach played defensive tackle before nearly ten thousand fans when the Cadets beat DeMatha, one of St. John's archrivals, to win our school's first Metro Conference football title since 1976. Offered a full scholarship by the 1986 national champion and perennial powerhouse Penn State Nittany Lions, Wayne Holmes was the only person I knew to play any sport at such an elite level. He was now one of St. John's football coaches, and the school was lucky to have him back.

That same afternoon I talked to Mark and Denise, I showed up at Coach Holmes's classroom after school. The door was open, and I heard music playing softly in the background. He sat at his desk grading papers while he hummed.

"Coach Holmes," I said. "I'm sorry to interrupt."

His pen stopped, and he turned to look at me, a kid who wanted to join something without being sure of exactly what he was getting into. Coach's long oval-of-chocolate face broke into an inquiring smile. Bald up top, he had the hair around his ears cut neat and close. Coach Holmes's desk seemed low to the ground. Even when he sat his height was imposing, and the width of his shoulders more so.

"What can I do for you, William?"

I was surprised. "You know my name?"

"Of course," he answered. "Many of us teachers, without having you in class, know that you're a good young man. You have a light about you."

My confidence lifted, but I wasn't sure what he meant. "I do?"

"Yes, we all do." Coach smiled. "You know the song," and he sang: "*This little light of mine, I'm gonna let it shine . . .*"

I had heard the cliché "a song in my heart," but Coach was the first person I had ever met for whom this was genuinely true. "Wow, that was beautiful."

"Much obliged." He placed the papers in a neat stack on his desk. "So what brings you by?"

"I've heard you're leading a gospel choir."

"You sing?"

"I like singing," I said, "especially in church, but that's the only place I've done it. As a worshiper, not a choir member."

Coach Holmes pushed back from his desk. He was thinking now, but the expression wasn't too different from the one that curtained his face when he sang. He was present with me in the room, but a piece of him was also elsewhere.

"How about this?" he asked. "Tomorrow afternoon the choir is meeting in my classroom. Show up and you can audition."

"So a tryout?"

"I mean come introduce yourself to your fellow choir members. Let them hear your voice! There are no outsiders in this room, William. Here, everyone belongs."

◆◆◆◆◆◆

The next afternoon when I entered Coach Holmes's classroom, the L.A. Mass Choir's "That's When You Bless Me" played and at least eight kids were present, including Mark and Denise. I was the last to arrive; maybe I was apprehensive. But the moment I walked in I felt the room shimmering with commitment.

"Anyone here want to tell William what this is all about?" Mr. Holmes began. Mark raised his hand, and Mr. Holmes nodded for him to go ahead.

"The first time I heard Coach's gospel music playing, I had to come in. I started coming here to listen to the music and to talk to Coach too. Denise started coming with me and one day we were just talking about how we can't do any of the things in school that we do when we're at home. So we asked Mr. Holmes if we could start a gospel choir and he said yes."

"How long have you been singing?" I asked Mark.

"I was four when I started singing in our church's children's choir."

"Four!" I marveled.

"I started singing around then too," Denise added. "Maybe I was five."

"William," Mr. Holmes said, "you have a song in mind you want to sing a few bars of?"

Nervous and without much of a gospel repertoire, I chose a song I still sing to my kids today: "Circle of Life" from *The Lion King*. I stood up straight and the song's first line came out of my mouth, then the second and the third. I could see that a note I hit, or tried to hit, sent a shudder through Coach Holmes. I paused.

"Should I keep going?"

"No," Coach Holmes answered. "We've heard enough. But I do have a question. How does singing make you feel?"

"Like I'm reaching out to something, something bigger than me."

Coach cocked his head. "You mean like . . . to God?" A moment of recognition passed between us. We were both saved.

I nodded. "Yes, exactly. To God."

I was not a great singer, but I had a good tone and, more important, was a believer and was enthusiastic, and the choir had room for that. "You're passionate, William. You have the spirit in your heart. Those two things, we can work with. Can't we, y'all?"

The choir members backed up Coach Holmes with a round of nods. Mark and Denise came over and hugged me, and the classroom had the warmth of the fellowship meal after church with Aunt Andrea and Uncle Steve. Only the sustenance was not food, but tolerance.

Though the St. John's student body was racially diverse, the institution itself, steeped in the tradition of the De La Salle Christian Brothers, a group of priests in the Catholic Church who serve exclusively as educators, was overtly patriarchal.

Sports dominated the school's culture, and the politics of the faculty and staff leaned heavily conservative. The students in the gospel choir included queer members, like Mark. Mr. Holmes had welcomed and embraced outsider kids with his open-door policy. Now, these kids who had been singing practically all their lives and who were generally outsiders at school accepted me, someone who had never before sung publicly, and who prior to this moment had spent all his time with the athletic kids. I wouldn't have put it this way then, but it was my faith and experience of never quite fitting in that inspired me to seek a place with these outsiders. Coach Holmes and the choir welcomed me, no questions asked. His classroom, as he said, was one where everyone belonged. Not just Christians and straight folks. Not just jocks and sports fans. But people of all religious persuasions, sexualities, and interests. The gospel choir was the first genuinely inclusive group I ever belonged to.

◆◆◆◆◆◆

"I need you to blend, William! Match the other voices! Match!" Coach Holmes instructed, and the more he told me to blend and match, match and blend, the better I listened to my fellow choir members.

"Inhale through your nose, exhale through your mouth. Instead of catching your breath, you should be singing with it!" I'd take the note and attempt to reroute my breath in choir practice, but focusing on my breath made me flub the lyrics. When I focused on the lyrics, I sang from my throat and quickly got out of breath.

One afternoon our rehearsal wrapped a few minutes early. Mark, Denise, and I stayed behind and were chatting with Coach Holmes when another history teacher, Mr. Hansen, popped his head in.

"Choir sounded great today."

"The kids work hard," Coach Holmes answered.

"Not as hard as you would have had to if you'd gone pro! Of course, you'd be raking in the millions."

Mark and Denise's faces turned to stone. I could see they didn't like what Mr. Hansen said.

"These young people are worth more than all the money in the world," Coach Holmes responded. "There's no place I'd rather be than here with them right now."

Mr. Hansen laughed. "You're one of a kind, Wayne. See you tomorrow."

It got quiet among the four of us. Since Coach Holmes matched and blended so well at the school, I wondered why he had not matched and blended with the NFL, the place everyone seemed to think he belonged. I had the impulse to ask him myself, but decided to let it go.

◆◆◆◆◆◆◆

In the years since I attended St. John's, the campus has undergone major renovations, including the opening of a state-of-the-art athletic facility. The place at my high school I have the most nostalgia for is one that no longer exists: the weight room. Though it looked bad and smelled worse, the workouts we got in there were nothing short of life changing. My junior and senior years, the same time I participated in the gospel choir, Coach Holmes trained me along with four or five other guys from the basketball team. In that musty room, literally coated with decades of young athletes' aspirations and dreams, even more than on the basketball court, I learned what I was made of.

We did circuit training, which targets specific muscles mainly on resistance equipment. Push-ups, sit-ups, lunges, abdominal exercises, and leg presses. I would focus on range-of-motion exercises, like leg lifts that build back and core strength. Mr. Holmes controlled the machine settings and the more force we exerted, the greater he set the resistance level. The faster we tried to complete the rep, the faster he cranked up the resistance.

My muscles throbbed under the strain, and my whole body shook with pain. But my mind focused on only one thing: not giving up. The heavier the weight, the greater the resistance. The narrower the range of motion, the more targeted the muscle group. When I thought I couldn't press on, or that I'd collapse or break if I did, Mr. Holmes would increase the pressure, the resistance, and shout like a righteous general in a just war, "Push! Push! Push! Don't stop! Don't give up on yourself! PUSH!"

I'd inhale, grit my teeth, and do as he said. My muscles threatened to give before they absorbed the pressure, converted the pressure to strength, and endured—to push more, push harder, push beyond. One moment I expected to fail. The next, I succeeded because Wayne Holmes told me I could, opening a doorway to inner power I wouldn't have known how to tap into on my own.

◆◆◆◆◆◆◆

My senior year, two Australian student-athletes named Luke Martin and Steve Leven traveled across hemispheres to enroll at St. John's and play basketball. Their coach in Sydney had attended St. John's decades earlier and was hoping that they could gain access to college scholarships by playing in the USA. Luke, about the same height as me at six feet, but with a slimmer build, was our starting point guard and Steve, at six feet four, a good shooter and very athletic, started at center. Over the next several months, I became close friends with Luke and when his living situation deteriorated, I asked if he and Steve wanted to come live at our house. Thankfully, my parents agreed and they both moved in, launching what would become a steady stream of more than twenty foreign students my parents would host, foster, or adopt after I graduated from high school.

Our team was the little engine that could. Small in traditional basketball terms, everyone was athletic and could handle the ball. Our pace was fast and aggressive, which complicated our opponents' transitions from offensive to defensive play and vice versa. We played small ball before it was popular, out of necessity.

The cocaptains were me, as starting power forward, and my buddy Jeff Palumbo, our starting shooting guard. Jeff was from a proud multigenerational Italian Catholic working-class family and at five feet eight, with a textbook jump shot, was the best shooter on the team. We had played together since we started as freshmen at St. John's and served as an anchoring force on our newly international team. Rounding out the starting five at small forward was Frank "Pete" Peterson. Six feet two and lean, Pete was a year younger than the rest of the starters and played with kinetic energy.

One of our assistant coaches, Austin Hatch, called me and Pete the pinky and the thumb. I, strong and stabilizing but short for a power forward, represented the thumb. Pete, wiry and sometimes off on his own, was the pinky. Coach Hatch would remind us that the hand doesn't function without the pinky and the thumb and that, though our other starting teammates were the remaining larger fingers and the leading scorers, they needed us to win. Coach Hatch repeated the catchphrase "The pinky and the thumb, gotta get it done," reminding us before every game of our vital role on the team.

Hours of practice, rain or shine, seven days a week, for

years built my skills and success as a player. I attended the storied Five-Star Basketball Camp, and Division I and II schools recruited me. My mother still has the letters and brochures from colleges around the country that flooded our mailbox for years in an oversize sack somewhere. But she knew nothing about the recruitment process, college athletics, or the likelihood of my success anywhere. Neither did Joseph. Neither did my father, Olayinka, who had joined the St. John's Men's Auxiliary, and attended every one of my games, cheering me on in a low-key way with nods and smiles, but rising to his feet and yelling at the ref when a call didn't go my way. For recruitment decisions, I relied on the expertise of coaches, especially Coach DeStefano, our head basketball coach, who everyone called Coach D.

At the beginning of my senior year, I asked Coach D. to meet with Mom, Joseph, and me. I wanted to know how I could best showcase myself to recruiters. We met in his office, the shelves lined with pictures going back decades. He greeted Mom and Joseph enthusiastically. Coach D. had gotten to know them well over the previous three seasons. Every season, Mom baked cookies for the players and the coaches too. She and Joseph took every bus trip and yelled the loudest at all the games. Joseph even took it upon himself to distribute water and towels to the team. Everyone loved my parents. I thought their presence might help me make my case for why I should play guard my senior year. Almost as soon as we sat down, Coach D., knowing exactly why we were there, said:

"You play forward on this team. That's where we need you." He leaned back in his office chair. "And Kathy, no cookies this season. Please." He laughed, patting his gut.

"Oh, Coach." Mom waved off his comment. I felt myself drifting out of my body. They were in one meeting and I was in another. I struggled to get the conversation back on track.

"But that's not where I need to be for the recruiters. I'm not tall enough to play forward anywhere but here," I said. "The right coaches won't look twice at me if they only see me play where the team needs me."

"Taking one for the team is a noble course of action. Anyhow, why worry? You'll get into a Division III school, no problem," Coach D. said. "That's a done deal."

"Coach, with all due respect it's Division III," I emphasized.

"That's where you belong, in a small school where you can thrive." He shot a glance at my mother and then Joseph. "The coach at Penn State Altoona loves you! I know you'll do great there. You'll have all the support you need."

"You think Altoona will give William a scholarship, right?" Joseph's eyes roved the coach's office, acknowledging the cost of St. John's. "We can hardly afford this place and our house, let alone a college tuition bill."

Mom nodded in assent. Coach D. assuaged their worries and exasperated mine. "Division III means he'll get a scholarship, no question."

The meeting was over. I couldn't understand how Mom and Joseph could be so involved with the team without being more involved in my individual life as a player, why they hadn't stood up for me. For the rest of the year, I did my best to put my feelings aside and played, for the team, as hard as I could. I understood that where college was concerned money heavily factored into Mom and Joseph's outlook. My recognition of that reality tempered my hurt.

❖❖❖❖❖❖❖

I had just finished a workout with Wayne and we were packing up for the day. It was probably a week or two after the meeting in Coach D.'s office.

"Where do you want to go to college?" he asked, seemingly out of the blue.

Instinct answered. "North Carolina Central, because that's where I can play basketball."

"You can play basketball at any park, any day of the week," Coach said. "And that's different from where you want to go to college."

I felt anger and self-pity rise up into my throat. "Coach D. won't let me play my real position and given my height and the fact that no one will recruit me to play forward, only Division III schools are interested. Division II at Central is the best I'm going to do."

"I understand." Coach Holmes's eyes focused squarely on mine. Different from the faraway look that took over when he sang, Coach's expression sparked presence and acuity. He had artist mode and coach mode, and in the choir the two mixed. Here, he enacted the artistry of a life coach, and ministered to me.

"But I didn't ask what Division you can go to. I asked what college *you* are interested in. You need to start thinking about college as its own thing, without basketball at the center of it. Pray for guidance toward that, William."

And I know, with hindsight, that he was right. A C student at the time, as far as I was concerned, I was studying basketball, and my classes were almost extracurricular.

Sometimes, after a bad game, I couldn't get out of bed the next day to attend school. I always gave my best, but my effort and my love of the game weren't always enough to guarantee a win. The combination of playing hard and losing was a poison to me then. My effort was little consolation. If we won, the team deserved the credit. If we lost, I was sure that I deserved the blame.

"I want to tell you something, Coach. The other day I

missed choir practice because I was so upset about the DeMatha game. I never made it to school."

"Yes . . ." He waited for me to continue.

"It wasn't because we lost. It was because I thought we were going to win, and then we didn't. It was the disappointment." I had never put those feelings into words before.

"Okay," he said. "Do you think anyone else felt as disappointed?"

"Of course. I know Jeff did. He said as much. The other guys didn't have to say a word. We all felt it."

"Did everyone else come to school the day after the game?"

"Yes."

"Then that was a win for them. Disappointment is a type of pressure. You can push through it."

◆◆◆◆◆◆◆

In February 2000, before a crowd of more than twenty-five hundred fans, I helped lead the St. John's Cadets to the Washington Catholic Athletic Conference championship game against our archrival, DeMatha. Having lost to them twice earlier in the season in close games, we were prepared for a challenge. Close for the entire game, we had our first and last lead early in the first half. With a little over a minute left in the game, our last chance to take the lead presented itself.

We were trailing 57–53, when my Aussie teammate Steve Leven hit a three-pointer from the corner, cutting the lead to 57–56. As DeMatha inbounded the ball and passed it toward half-court, I jumped in front to intercept the pass and pushed the ball ahead to Pete, who found Luke in the corner for another three-pointer, putting us ahead 59–57, with fifty-nine seconds left to play.

Being the great team that they were, DeMatha wasn't

done. Their star guard Billy Edelin, who would later win an NCAA Division I national championship at Syracuse University with his teammate and future NBA star Carmelo Anthony, hit a running layup with forty-five seconds left to tie the game at 59–59.

We advanced the ball and my cocaptain, Jeff Palumbo, got it at half-court with thirty seconds remaining. He held it there and glanced up at the clock, allowing it to run down so we would take the last shot. No matter what, we were at least going to overtime. Seconds ticked off, ten, nine, eight, seven— then Jeff made his move to the basket. He drove right, looked at me briefly on the baseline, and then threw up a floater with 1.6 seconds remaining. It rolled on the rim for what seemed like an eternity and dropped in the basket! We had done it. We'd knocked off Goliath and won the championship. Our fans stormed the court and chanted, "S-J-C, S-J-C, S-J-C!"

I have an amazing wife and four children whom I love dearly. After my wedding day and the births of my children, this moment stands among the happiest of my life.

◆◆◆◆◆◆◆

The memory of feeling abandoned by my mother and Joseph in Coach D.'s office was so strong that when the time came for me to start training at North Carolina Central my freshman year, I asked Coach Holmes if he would drive with me. My parents had cheered for me from the stands, but they could offer me no guidance about my athletic career. Nervous about the transition, I needed the man who taught me to push to help ferry me into this next phase. If I had no qualms about asking Coach, it was because I had nowhere else to turn. By God's grace, he agreed. Years later, when I asked him why he came with me, his answer was simple. "I could be there for you, so I was."

In the car, we played gospel for nearly three hundred miles of highway on I-95 South. Cracker Barrels and rest stops became horse farms and vegetable sellers before becoming Cracker Barrels and rest stops again. A song that he associated with his girlfriend must have come on, because unexpectedly Coach mentioned that he was dating a woman named Aisha whom he liked a lot and was considering marrying. That he shared this about himself edged us from a close student-teacher dynamic to the beginnings of a friendship.

"Does Aisha like sports, gospel, or both, Coach?"

"Aisha enjoys both." He paused for a moment. "And something I'd enjoy is if you called me Wayne."

A rush of pride straightened my spine. "Alright, *Wayne*," I said, suddenly feeling grown-up, like I was actually ready for college. Wayne let out a chuckle, turned up the music, and returned to singing. I tried to blend my voice with his, but it was hard. Wayne's voice was beautiful, and for a lot of the ride I just listened to this wonderful man who seemed like he'd figured out how to exist in peace and confidence.

We headed to the gym the moment we arrived on Central's verdant campus. Few students were back yet, making the campus resemble a set more than an actual lived-in place, which unfortunately captures my experience there. I thought I had a guaranteed role on the basketball team. It turned out I was little more than an extra.

The coach who had recruited me and seen a place for me on the team had taken another job at a different school. The new coach had chosen his own players and I clearly wasn't one of them. While not barring me from showing up, he made it known that my chances of making the team were slight. I could come to preseason workouts and practices and work as hard as I wanted. That was on me. But he made no promises about my actually playing.

Wayne dropped me off at my dorm and he did not mince words. "William, you're on borrowed time down here. You need something other than basketball to focus on. There's much more to life than sports, much more." He stood before me like a sage oak tree.

"Pray on it, William. Ask God what He wants for you. Not just what you think you want. I think there's something other than basketball for you. Sports take us places and show us things about ourselves. The point of playing is seeing those things. That's the real sport. Life is the real sport."

I heard Wayne, but I refused to listen. Life may have been the real sport, but my life, at this point, was basketball. "I'm going to push down here, just like you taught me. I think I can do it. I think I can earn a place on the team."

Wayne was thoughtful for a moment. "Just make sure you're pushing in the right direction. I'm praying on it for you," he said before getting in his car and heading back to Maryland.

❖❖❖❖❖❖❖

I participated in all the preseason workouts and the guys on the team were nice enough, but I should have understood this as the death knell. They felt sorry for me. They knew what I refused to let myself believe. At the official start of the season, I didn't even get a spot on the bench.

Without the discipline of basketball, my days seemed pointless. My classes didn't interest me, nothing did, so I passed the time going to parties and hanging out with girls. One night I called Wayne.

"What are you thinking—you going back down there next semester?" he asked.

"No."

Wayne's silence filled the phone line but I knew there was no judgment there. "I'm not saying that you'll never play basketball again, but you need to start thinking about what you want to do other than basketball, where you really want to go to college."

My days of ROTC involvement back at St. John's popped into my head. St. John's had one of the oldest high school Reserve Officer Training Corps programs in the country, and while I liked the volunteer work mostly because I liked the girls in uniforms, some time wallowing, depressed, made it clear that I liked volunteering because it wasn't about me, but about serving someone else. I had done Big Brother–like basketball clinics with elementary school kids as a high school student. Maybe instead of being a student, it was time to be of service.

"I've had enough of college for the time being," I answered.

I thought about how Wayne had driven me down to Central for no other reason than to give me the support I needed. I thought about the man at Christian camp who had held me through my Holy Ghost experience. I wanted to be like these men. That's what I needed: a life less about me and more about other people.

"I want to help people," I said. "That's what I want to do. Help people."

"Let's look at volunteer programs." Wayne didn't miss a beat. "I'll email you what I come up with. In the meantime, you start looking, too."

About a week later, I submitted an AmeriCorps application. The organization had come up in Wayne's search and mine. I called home to tell my mother and she delivered some unexpected news. She and Joseph had decided to sell the house in Beltsville. They had moved there mostly for me, and now that I was in college they wanted to relocate to rural Manchester in the northernmost part of the state, a few miles from the Pennsylvania border. Their mortgage and taxes had started to erode their budget for essentials like groceries. The farther they moved from DC, the farther their money would go. It was the right decision for them, but it put me in a whole other bind.

"Mom, I don't want to stay down here at Central," I admitted.

She answered sympathetically, wanting to make it better. "Come home then, William."

"How's that going to work?" My question betrayed my feelings of abandonment. "I've applied to AmeriCorps in Silver Spring. Now you're going to live sixty miles away."

"We can figure something out," Mom answered. I wasn't so sure. After we hung up, I called Wayne and told him that my parents were moving.

"Let me talk about it with Aisha, but I think when you come back you can live with me."

"You do?" I asked, ecstatic.

He answered without hesitation in his smooth, deep voice. "Yes. Aisha likes you. So do I."

❖❖❖❖❖❖

In 2001, the year of the 9/11 terrorist attacks, when my love of country had never been stronger, and while I was living with Wayne, the Montgomery County Police pulled me over ten different times.

During that time of officers stopping me again and again without cause, I was actually working *for* the Montgomery County Police Department on my AmeriCorps assignment. I logged evidence, filed police reports, and occasionally dressed up as McGruff the Crime Dog at school events. After the third time I got pulled over, I took to wearing my police ID on a lanyard around my neck every time I got behind the wheel. It worked: as soon as officers noticed it, they would let me go. At the time, I was seriously considering a career in law enforcement, but this experience of working for the police while simultaneously being racially profiled and targeted by them forced me to reappraise why I made the decision to join AmeriCorps and work for the police in the first place.

In a matter of months, I had traveled the distance from high school basketball star riding high on championship glory to dumped college recruit sitting on the sidelines. The mainspring of my identity was wrapped around basketball, and without it I searched for another way to be in the world. I wanted to get over myself, out of my skin. Yet, the police stops were literally about me, *and my skin*, and the paradox of yearning to serve while being a casualty of a common racist practice made it clear that law enforcement was not my path.

The first time I got pulled over by the Montgomery County Police, I was listening to "He's Able" by Kirk Franklin. The flashing red lights and the whir of the siren behind me worked like a fist closing around my heart. I put on my blinker and pulled onto the shoulder. I hadn't been speeding. I had no idea why I was being pulled over, other than that I was a young Black man with cornrows driving an SUV.

One of the talks Joseph gave me from the time he started dating my mother was how to conduct myself in an encounter with a police officer. He instructed me to move slowly and deliberately. He explained how I should be extremely polite and respectful, like he had once suggested I be with a white racist teacher. Millions of Black parents repeatedly instruct their children, especially their boys, on how to act, what to do, what to say, and not say, in such an encounter. Deference to an officer can save a young man's life. But this deference also feels so much like groveling. Without being fully conscious of it, I chose another way, one Wayne had taught me.

I turned the volume on my music very low, but I didn't turn it off. I had sung "He's Able" as a solo at my high school graduation, and practiced it with Wayne for weeks, focusing on controlling my breath by keeping my shoulders still and breathing deeply from my diaphragm. I found myself doing the same thing now, trying to keep myself breathing steadily.

I was polite. So was the officer. When nothing came up against my license and registration, he let me go. But he never told me why he had pulled me over. In the world of pretextual stops where officers use minor traffic violations as the pretense for investigating those they suspect of serious crimes because of their race or ethnicity, he didn't have to. Through it all, I controlled my breath, just as Wayne had taught me.

◆◆◆◆◆◆◆

I tried to pay Wayne rent money. When he refused to take it, I bought food and household essentials, and cleaned. Wayne never told me to cheer up or that everything was going to be alright when I stayed in and stared at *SportsCenter* for nights in a row. No home. No scholarship. No basketball. For a kid who fell in love with basketball from the first time he made a layup pass, life seemed pretty bleak. But Wayne refused to let me give up.

Instead, he would turn the television off, turn gospel on, and sing as he organized his work for the next day. On Friday and Saturday nights, Aisha came over and we stayed up late listening to music and talking. The music ministered to me and so did Wayne and Aisha. With their help, I started to put my life back together, and decided to stay in the DC area and attend Catholic University for the upcoming fall semester. Their coach had been interested in me in high school, so maybe he still would be now.

It must have been after midnight on a Friday. Aisha fell asleep on the couch, and Wayne had just scrambled us a few eggs for a late-night snack. As a Fred Hammond record played, it felt like we were out at a diner, not sitting in Wayne's kitchen.

"How did you do it?" I asked.

Wayne looked confused. It was late and I was being vague, unsure that I wasn't out of line to mention his derailed football career. "Recover from not being able to go pro?" I clarified. I had spent months sulking about not playing college ball and now I began to wonder even more deeply how Wayne had managed not to be defeated by disappointment when people still, years later, reminded him that there was another, better future that could have been his—a future with money, fame, and accolades.

Wayne was quiet for a minute before he answered. This was one thing we had never spoken about directly.

"Nothing is guaranteed, especially when you are an athlete, as you well know. That's doubly true if you're a football player."

"But how did you deal with it? Going pro was everything that you worked for."

"A pro career is not what I worked toward. It's what other people assumed was the ultimate goal for me. But it wasn't my end goal."

"Why not?" Was it possible that Wayne himself had been in a situation where he was thwarted, where he couldn't manage to push hard enough to make it through?

"It was July, hot," Wayne started, "the summer before my freshman year and I had just moved into the dorms at Penn

State. We had a Kickoff Classic game against Georgia Tech, my very first for the team. Right off, I hurt my back in the scrimmage. The doctor examined it. Said it didn't look good, that I had to sit out.

"I went back to the dorms beside myself but thinking I would be back in for the next game. Then the recruitment coach showed up and said I was sitting out that entire semester."

"The semester?" I was shocked. "But you'd just got there?"

"That's right. And I packed my suitcase and got in his Ford Taurus. The flight from State College back to BWI was about thirty minutes. The drive home from the airport was another thirty minutes. No more than four hours had passed since I got hurt. The semester hadn't even started and I was back home. Let me tell you, William—for a moment, it looked grim.

"But then I took two or three classes at Montgomery College. I kept my head down. I did my work and I prayed. In December, the coach called me out of the blue and said they wanted me back. Just like that, I returned to Penn State. And I played all four years, right up until I injured my back again, right before graduation. It's strange, but God showed me at the beginning of my time at Penn State more or less what the end would be. None of the time between the beginning and the end was ever promised. That's what God prepared me for. Not to go pro, but to live a real life after football was over, a life of service. To know that my time as an athlete was borrowed, nothing more."

"Who supported you through all this? Your parents?"

A sad, stony smile stretched across Wayne's face. "My father came to every single one of my high school practices. Everyone thought he was so supportive, that he turned his schedule inside out to be there for me. Do you want to know why he really came?"

The growing tension in Wayne's voice made me nervous. I hesitated. "Why?"

"So he could tell me about every mistake I made, everything that I did wrong. That's what my father did to me. He was even worse with my mother. Yet, when he died, we mourned him."

The shock of Wayne's testimony left me speechless. Since I had lived with him, I had started to attend church with him and his mother, Mrs. Holmes, who I came to call Momma Holmes. She was one of the kindest and most special women I had ever met. At Wayne's wedding I walked her down the aisle. With her being a professional baker and an excellent cook, there was not a hungry person or grieving person in Momma Holmes's sphere that she did not serve and care for with many meals over weeks and sometimes months. Momma Holmes was the kind of woman who gave everything she had and then prayed for more so that she could give that away too. Two of the most caring people I had ever met had lived for years with an abuser?

"My father was one of my best teachers because he taught me everything not to do, how not to be a role model, what never to say to a young person you want to see do well."

"But you did well, Wayne. How?"

"I had my mother and I had my faith and it was me on the football field, not him. I was my own person and I decided that I wasn't going to let my father define me."

Wayne leaned back against the couch, took a deep breath, and started to sing along with the album, "*No weapon formed against me shall prosper, it won't work.*"

5

DEEN SANWOOLA

IN THE AFTERMATH OF THE NIGERIAN CIVIL WAR, DURING the summer of 1972, my father left his home in Ibadan for the States to study on an academic scholarship. He returned home for the first time more than thirty-three years later in 2005, with my fiancée, Michele, and me. Deen Sanwoola, the IT systems manager I met at my mother's office, BPI, traveled back and forth between the States and Nigeria four or five times a year, and from the time I met him as a child of ten in 1993, he urged me to visit Nigeria and see more of the world, so I might see more of myself.

My mother's production role at BPI developed into her overseeing aspects of the office's general operations, and she met with Deen, who managed the server, every other week. I sometimes tagged along with Mom to the meetings, in awe of this Black man who understood and held within his control the entire functionality of the office. Deen was like the Wizard of Oz. Only there was no curtain or pretending, just his brilliance at managing computers.

Deen could provide you with a rundown of environmental controls and infrastructure, ranging from fire suppression to airflow patterns. Trained in servers, Deen understood computer hardware, programming, and networking systems. The server room itself, nests of yellow, black, and red cords and tiny pulsating green lights, was like something out of a science-fiction movie for most people back in the early nineties. A lucky kid, I got to see up close the fiber optic guts of the world we live in today. At the center of that world, there was, coincidentally, a young Nigerian man. It cannot be underestimated how much of a role coincidence plays in the acquisition of Black fathers, as well as other things that are out of our control, like demographic shifts and where you happen to get a job. My mother met Joseph because of her position at BPI, where I also met Jay and Deen. But my parents moved to Montgomery County where BPI was located in the early 1980s because of the area's reputation as a diverse and economically thriving place, on the doorstep of the nation's capital.

In 1960, the foreign-born population in Montgomery County hovered under 5 percent. Data from the 2020 census puts that number at around 36 percent. My father was part of this decades-long wave of immigration that reconfigured Montgomery County as an international community. So was Kalfani's family and so many more. Deen prompted me to go beyond casually observing this phenomenon to understanding that I, as a global citizen, was a part of it. Deen set my sights on horizons well beyond the Washington, DC, area, which, as someone who entered politics at a young age and is from the DC metro area, gives me much-needed perspective. Montgomery County was a place where the world, in my lifetime at least, was arriving, departing, and returning every day while my father merely watched it go by, stuck. Much of the perspective Deen gave me concerned my Nigerian identity and my father's depression, which I now understand I was mired in too.

For years, I had unknowingly conflated my father's emotional distance with what it meant to be Nigerian. I had so few consistent ties with my Nigerian family and after the divorce no other models for who Nigerians were. Until I met Deen, I thought being Nigerian was to be *like* my father. My mother's whiteness had a midwestern, salt of the earth specificity to it, born of her Kansas background. When she changed my name, she stripped the Blackness I inherited from my father of its Nigerian-ness. The binary of Black and white became the lens through which I viewed so much of my experience. But Deen reminded me that I wasn't just Black and white, that was way too simplistic. I was American and Nigerian, too. And to be a Nigerian was not to exist on a spectrum of clinical depression, stranded and struggling in America, a victim of a "dream deferred" as Langston Hughes put it. The Nigerian identity instead meant energy, resilience, hustle, and the entrepreneurial spirit that put dynamic figures, like Deen, on the international stage.

It's commonly said that the Beltway is not the whole country. Yet for many in the political sphere, the Beltway *is* the world. Deen's influence on me as a young man ensured that I would not fall into that trap. I may have inherited my Nigerian heritage from my father, and my relationship with him may have been strained, but Deen's friendship and mentorship made me aware that I belonged to the Nigerian diasporic community.

◆◆◆◆◆◆◆

My father's links to Nigerians here in the States were sparse. The one exception I can recall is from the time I was little, before my parents divorced. Back then, my father saw a lot of his best friend and first cousin, Uncle Tunde, who like Dad was a Nigerian transplant in the DC metro area.

Uncle Tunde and his wife, Aunt Simi, both nurses, lived in Laurel, about twenty minutes from Silver Spring, in a neat apartment complex that was always bustling with food and family. They had three kids, the only Nigerian cousins I had access to, and they were all within five years of my age. I have memories of running around their house in an endless game of tag as the jollof rice cooked and the gamy goat egusi soup scented the air with onions and a feeling of heartiness—of something elemental. Raised on her mother's Austrian-influenced cuisine, infused with the influence of Betty Crocker cookbooks that she then carried into her own kitchen, Mom made delicious meals, though a lot of the starches started in boxes, and she seasoned them with packets, not fresh herbs. While my mother's style of cooking had been invented by midcentury American food scientists, the recipes for Uncle's traditional Nigerian meals had come down through oral traditions. Food at Uncle Tunde's wasn't just for your body. He also cooked for the spirit yearning for home.

I never hung around the adults for long spells at Uncle Tunde's. My father and Uncle Tunde wouldn't have allowed it, and I didn't want to anyway. But how I remember them standing together laughing and smiling in the kitchen, or intently listening to each other as they sat side by side on the living room sofa, says to me now that they were not men who talked and listened to each other to find out what occurred in each other's life as much as men who talked to each other because they *already knew* what had happened. There was a certainty, a shared conviction in their Nigerian stories. The American ones were much more fragile.

After my parents divorced, we saw Uncle Tunde and my cousins Wale, Jummi, and Dapo less often, though they were the most consistent presence of my Nigerian family and a bright and healing salve for me, joining us for graduations and other important events. It would have made sense for my father to have taken me over to Uncle Tunde's instead of to Roy Rogers during our Sunday visits. That way we could have experienced community together. We could have been father and son in a community of friends and fellow countrymen. But

Dad's shame all too often cut him off from the healing power of fellowship. My mother's agency and volition, that she initiated the divorce and that my father ultimately folded to her demands, embarrassed him. The fact that Uncle Tunde was a fellow Nigerian, I suspect, only amplified Dad's humiliation despite any advice or kind words his cousin may have shared.

◆◆◆◆◆◆◆

Though I was too young to remember, I met my Nigerian grandmother, Alhaja Taibat Jawando, only once, when I was six months old and she visited us in Maryland. After that visit, only confirmed for me through pictures, we would speak a couple of times a year on the phone.

The daughter of a respected, wealthy man in Lagos, my grandmother traveled to Mecca for the hajj in the 1950s, which was rare for a woman and even rarer for a Black Nigerian one. My grandmother stood apart from other women and many of the men in her community. My grandfather, who sought a political career in Ibadan's Muslim community, pursued a match with my grandmother as a stepping-stone toward his own ambitions. He succeeded in marrying her, and, granted access to my grandmother's family's political connections, he established his own. A community pillar in her own right, my grandmother had a life of comfortable prominence. All the same, international calls stretched the phone lines in the area of Ibadan where she lived to their limits, and when we talked the crackle of the connection featured more prominently than either of our voices or her strong Yoruba accent. I'd press the receiver to my ear, yearning to hear her soft voice shrunk to a halting whisper by the buzzing connection cutting in and out.

"*Bawo ni*, how are you?" she'd say. *Bawo ni* is "how are you" in Yoruba, as she would often mix both languages.

"I'm fine," I'd answer wistfully. "How are you?" My voice would crack, tears seeping from my eyes. I longed to see her, touch her hands, and feel her embrace. I wanted to hear her voice clearly and observe how her mouth moved when she talked, and if the expression in her eyes matched her words.

"I," she'd say, and then for a moment the sound would drop until it returned with "for you." I assumed she had said, "I pray for you." I prayed for her too—that she would remain healthy long enough for me to meet her again and that I would remember every moment of our reunion this time. That somehow all the miles and years between us could be bridged. "I love you, Yemi," she'd say.

"I love you, Grandma."

I missed my grandmother without really knowing her. I missed her so deeply because I held out hope that she could connect me to the Nigerian identity that I felt my father had severed me from. I wanted to see for myself the fathoms of her life written on her countenance, the soul of her work in this world etched into her hands.

As a Black boy, I needed my Black fathers—as this book testifies to on nearly every page. All of us Black boys do. Undoubtedly, we also need our Black mothers. Aunt Andrea, Joseph's sister-in-law, fulfilled that role partially, but my grandmother's absence cut deeply. I felt she carried pieces of me within her that only a grandmother's love and warmth could unlock. I blamed my father for my not knowing her, and I felt because I didn't know her that a vital piece of my Nigerian heritage would always be beyond my reach.

◆ ◆ ◆ ◆ ◆ ◆ ◆

Mom later told me that she never asked Deen if he was okay with me hanging around after their server room meetings because she could tell by how he greeted me, with a laugh that made me want to laugh, too, how much he enjoyed our talks.

For years, Deen made sure he hit one subject in each of our conversations: Nigeria.

He always talked about how lucky American kids and families were because in Nigeria, where he had grown up on the outskirts of Ikorodu, only children from the most fortunate families attended school. In rural communities, parents and siblings pooled their own money to pay the teachers, in addition to tuition. This was out of reach for most Nigerian families.

Deen reminisced about the first time he had ever seen a computer in what amounted to the pop-up office of a trucking company that transported fish and produce from Ikorodu to the heart of Lagos. He fell in love with the bright green numbers, letters, and symbols displayed on the dark screen, which resembled a riddle from another world that he would discover was American in origin. If I wanted to truly appreciate the bounty of my American life, and recognize how remarkable America was, visit Nigeria, Deen would say. If I wanted to understand the source of the strength and energy he said drummed inside of me, I had to visit Nigeria, the place of my father's birth. "You will love *our* country," he exclaimed, "just *love* it." He really sat on that one-syllable word, his eyes lit up with certainty. "One day you'll go, and you'll see for yourself that I'm right."

At Christmastime, we always traveled to see Mom's family in Kansas. Outside of that annual trip, we rarely left the DC area. This made the thought of traveling to Nigeria seem like sheer fantasy, like it belonged to someone else's life. I could imagine boarding the silver plane and little else. "I would like to get there one day," I said, knowing little of Africa except for the few things I learned on National Geographic shows about the savanna, and that it was the place my father was from, and my grandmother's home.

As I talked with Deen, I'd often think about my grandmother and how sweet and tender her voice was, but then the distant presence of my father would fill my mind. Why didn't he visit Nigeria? Why didn't he want to take me to meet his relatives? Didn't he miss his mother and the rest of his family? His father, my grandfather, had died several years before I was born. Did that have anything to do with why he hadn't returned home? Certainly, his mother mattered more to him than the fact that people may have judged his life in America. But Dad prized what he thought of himself above the opinion of others. Unfortunately, his opinion of his own self-worth was at times very low. Deen was similar to my father in that he also prized his own opinion above that of other people. The difference between Deen and my father was that Deen thought highly of himself.

Younger than my father, Deen had already surpassed him professionally. From a background that teetered on the underclass, Deen had known since he was a kid that he had to be scrappy. Dad, on the other hand, from a wealthier family, felt like he had been scrapped by his father who had added another wife, according to Muslim custom, by the time he was born. But as the youngest of her four children, Dad was also his mother's favorite child, maybe because he represented the last of my grandparents' marriage.

Without a family history to hinder him, Deen scrambled up the ladder of social and economic mobility toward a future that seemed of its own making. On the brink of the twenty-first century's internet revolution, Deen used his American salary to finance his businesses in Nigeria, where at one time he owned an internet café in Lagos, while he also ran an import operation. When you're a kid you accept labels like "business-man" without understanding what commerce is, how it works, or what it takes to succeed at business. Part of why I ended up knowing so little about Deen's endeavors is because I met him as a child. Just like it's hard for any kid to really imagine that their teacher has a life outside of school, even though Deen constantly talked about Nigeria, not only was it difficult for me to imagine what the country was actually like, it was also equally hard to wrap my mind around what kind of work he did there, outside of the server room at BPI. As I got older my curiosity about the details of Deen's business did not grow, even as my connection with him deepened.

"How often do you return to Nigeria?" I asked, awed that he returned at all.

"As often as is required," he answered, his mind captured by the string of symbols on the screen.

"Required?" I questioned.

"Yes." He looked directly at me and smiled. "I have a life and lots of work here in the States. I also have a life and work in Nigeria. The two are connected. Do you see that, William? By me." He laughed and stretched his arms out at his sides as if his limbs themselves could link two continents, which is in fact what his presence did in my life. "Sometimes I am required to be in one place more than the other. On average, I go there five or six times a year."

I'm not sure I went to DC five or six times a year back then. "How long does it take to get there?"

"You mean the flight? With a good connection, about four-teen hours."

"Fourteen hours?!" I was shocked.

Deen laughed again and copied something down from the screen on a yellow legal pad. "Hey, to travel to the other side of the world in fourteen hours is pretty good."

"Aren't your lives in the US and Nigeria way different?" I asked.

"Both places are part of me, they are in my blood," Deen said, without lifting his eyes from the screen. "And the hustle in both places, it's crazy exciting. Life is a hustle, William. But if you meet the challenge by doing the hard work, your life will be sweet." Deen ever so lightly licked his lips, which broke into another horizon-wide smile. "I can taste life. I want you to taste it too."

"Does it taste like wires, plastic, and metal like all the stuff in this room?"

"Not at all," Deen said. "It tastes like a sugar cube melting on your tongue on a perfect day."

Deen had a giant cell phone that resembled a walkie-talkie from the 1950s on the table beside the desktop where he worked. Over the years, that single huge phone became three or four small ones. Deen was multitasking and distracted before distraction became a thing. From his phones, the hustle reached out to him like it does to many of us now. And the hustle meant one of two things: you were either solving problems or making money. Deen loved doing both, applying the technology of connectivity and information to logistics: transporting objects, getting people what they needed in far-off places, and helping people connect across oceans to solve problems together. The sweetness Deen spoke of was the interrelatedness of the world.

"Have you ever been off American soil?" he asked.

I was eleven or twelve at the time and answered, "No. We're not rich. We don't have money for that."

"Do you at least *dream* of trying new things?" Deen questioned playfully.

"At school, the only *new things* anyone ever talks about are drugs and we're told to say no to those."

Deen laughed, hard. I knew he wasn't talking about drugs,

but at that moment I had to be a smart aleck. It was the only way I knew to keep my head up in the conversation. Deen was no smart aleck, he was just smart.

"Traveling around the world, making money, and helping people can feel like a drug, a medicine," Deen said, his eyes still glued to the screen.

"How?" I wanted to know.

"It's chemistry," Deen answered. "Traveling and working, seeing Africa, these are things that could change not the chemistry of your body, but of your mind and of your life."

"What exactly is chemistry really?" For one week in science class, we discussed chemistry, but all I got from the lessons was that there were physical changes and then there were chemical ones. The physical alterations were ones that could be observed, while the chemical ones were invisible.

Deen struck a few keys on his laptop and briefly studied his smaller screen before checking out something on a desktop terminal. Freeing a little more space in his brain, he finally answered. "Chemistry is the science of change and energy. When there's a change, energy either gets released or absorbed."

"The change I want is to see my grandmother!" I said, suddenly on the brink of tears. "When I think of Nigeria, all I can see is her. In my head, my grandmother *is* Nigeria."

Deen turned away from the screen and gave me his full attention for the first time during our conversation. "Grandmothers are like countries because they are where we come from." The laughter left Deen's eyes. "All our grandmothers are our source. I hope you meet yours, William. I do. Going to Nigeria, where your father is from, and seeing your grandmother, it will change your energy. It will change you."

My curiosity was piqued. "How?"

But Deen had reached his limit. "William, I could answer

your questions from today till tomorrow but you will still need to visit Nigeria to find out."

◆◆◆◆◆◆◆

Over the years that followed I thought a lot about change and energy where my father was concerned. He moved from apartment to apartment, but somehow each new place seemed exactly like the one before. The buzzers never worked and the buildings all had leaky radiators and heating issues. The scent of marijuana floated in the hallways, often masking the stench of garbage. His apartments consisted of bare walls that needed to be painted and worn carpet made dingier still by the absence of furniture. My father had a sofa, two chairs, a table, a bed, and a stereo. By most people's standards, he lived like a monk. By my standards, ones that my chats with Deen had inevitably shaped, Dad lived like a man without hustle.

For months after Mom and Joseph bought their house in Beltsville, my father never once said a word about it. My freshman year at St. John's, as he drove me home one Sunday night, I was so annoyed, I brought up the subject.

"Are you ever going to congratulate Mom on buying a new house?"

Dad's silence filled the car. I rolled down my window to release some of the tension, and to get some fresh air. Since the conversation was heating up, the sharp chill felt good.

"Did you hear me?" I asked, an edge in my voice. "Why haven't you at least mentioned it?"

Twenty or thirty seconds passed, an eternity in a conversation with my father. "I'm driving *you* there now. Isn't that enough for you?" The question was serrated. What cut was how Dad said "*you.*"

"No, it's not enough." My resolve deepened. "You should say something to Mom. Strangers have congratulated us on the house. It's the least she could expect from the father of her son."

"What should I say? *I couldn't give you this, so you got it with another man* . . ." Dad's eyes remained fixed on the road ahead, his grip so tight on the steering wheel that the color bled from his knuckles. I thought I'd brought this up because I wanted him to be more respectful of my mother. It turned out I also wanted him to be more respectful of himself.

"Why can't you find better places to live?" I asked. "All the places you live—" I cut myself off and started again. "Why do you always . . ." I searched for a word. "Settle? Do you want to die in a place like your apartment?"

Something nearer to stoicism than complacency deflated his anger. "I live where I can afford the rent. Where my work allows me. When the contract ends, so does my position. Other contract hires get extended. I'm left waiting for a new contract somewhere different every time."

Was he a bad worker? Or was it just that the friendlier guys got better results? Did Dad do a good job but get cut because he went under the radar? I guessed it was the latter, and I thought of Deen. Deen got along so well with my mother, who was his liaison at BPI. They treated each other as pure equals. Was it that people treated my father as inferior, as a subordinate at the agencies where he got work, because of the color of his skin or his Nigerian accent? Did he show how that treatment made him feel, the way he showed how it pained him that he couldn't buy my mother a house? Was that why he wasn't asked to return? His smoldering disappointment in his American life? Dad was a good worker and smart. He just wasn't a good pretender.

Dad pulled up in front of our little middle-class dream home in Beltsville with its attached garage and boxwood bushes. But he didn't so much as glance at the house. Instead, he fixed his gaze on me. "See you next week, Yemi."

"Alright, Dad." I began rolling up the window before getting out of the car.

"No, leave it," he said, rolling down the window on the driver's side. "I could use the air."

◆◆◆◆◆◆◆

I was at home in the kitchen when the phone rang. Mom spoke for a minute, then brought me the handset. The skin at the corner of her eyes looked red, bruised. She wasn't crying, but something was wrong.

"It's your father," she said. I nervously took the phone, wondering what Dad had done now, or failed to do.

"Hello."

"It's your grandmother," my father said, grief splintering his voice. "She's dead." I held the phone away, refusing to believe what I'd heard. My mother rubbed my back in a circular motion like she used to at bedtime when I was small.

"It's not true. I just talked to her a few days ago."

"She's gone, Yemi. My mother, your grandmother, is gone."

Mom continued to rub my back and whispered, "I'm sorry, William," and I flinched when I heard my American name. The sound of *William* coming out of her mouth, triggered by my grandmother's death, set something off within me. Just as I was registering the loss of my Nigerian grandmother, my body remembered that my mother had changed my Nigerian name.

"When are we leaving for her funeral?" I asked.

"We're not," Dad said, his voice stiff, like he was a hostage under threat of torture. I realize now that he was. He was held captive by his impossible pride.

"We're not?! Why?" I cried. "We've got to be there for her."

"It's Muslim tradition to be buried within forty-eight hours. I can't afford a ticket to get there in time." The line clicked. Dad had hung up. And something in me shut down on my father.

Couldn't he have asked for a loan from his brother, my wealthy uncle Segun? Couldn't he have found a way? What he couldn't afford was his pride. How could he ever make peace with his mother's death if he didn't attend her funeral? How could I? I had always feared that my grandmother would die before I could experience her embrace. What I never imagined was that after she did pass, my father would not have the funds or emotional resources to figure out a way to say his final goodbye, and that, as a result, neither would I.

I found myself wanting to talk to Deen, to tell him that my grandmother had passed, and that my father couldn't do what most anyone would have done in that situation: return home. Dad's reaction to the death of his mother, more than anything else during those years, expressed the depth of his clinical depression. Depression sucked his energy, which made him more depressed. It was a vicious cycle. Asking his brother for a loan, doing something, anything, would have taken too much energy for my father, energy his depression had long since evaporated. As much as I wanted to tell Deen about my grandmother and my father, the undertow of shame pulled me close to that low place where my father subsisted. Unlike my father, Deen would have found a way. Deen would have hustled. I wasn't sure that I myself could have found a way. Confronting my own helplessness, I feared I was more like my father than Deen.

❖❖❖❖❖❖

By the early 2000s, about five years after my grandmother died, Deen was spending more time in Nigeria than in the States, and had quit his job at BPI. I didn't ask questions about the nature of his visits back and forth or why he left the publishing firm, figuring either the position didn't pay enough or that he didn't need the money anymore. While I was still a student at North Carolina Central, Deen mentioned in an email that he had opened an internet café back home. Once, when he was in DC, where I was now a student at Catholic University, he sent me another email with the address of an internet café near Dupont Circle, and the date and time that he would be there. I figured he was sizing up the place in an effort to tweak his internet café in Lagos and thought it would be nice if I joined him. The minute I walked in Deen waved me over, yet his eyes seemed glued to his laptop, as usual. Before I sat down, Deen said, "You're a Jawando man now."

"That's a funny way to start a conversation."

"Then tell me how old you are now," said Deen.

"Nineteen," I answered.

"That means your parents can't make your decisions anymore."

"Yes . . . but what kinds of decisions do you mean?"

"When you were younger, I would have needed your parents' permission to take you to Nigeria. Now that you're older, all you have to say is yes."

"Yes to what," I asked, "credit card debt?" Much like my father, my reflexive response was, "No way I can afford a ticket to Nigeria." I had also inherited some of my father's shame. Whether I had the money or not, I'm not sure, without Deen, I would have felt entitled or even imagined I was good enough, or *Nigerian* enough, to go.

"I'll pay your airfare," Deen said, flashing his pearly white teeth as he turned the computer screen toward me. "Why didn't you tell me who your uncle was?"

"My uncle?" I was trying to get my bearings, as I began to read what Deen had clearly devoured. It was a biography of my father's brother, Uncle Segun, prominently featuring the number of government posts he had occupied from the 1970s onward, on a site detailing the attendees at a conference held in London. Uncle Segun's most conspicuous position was "Permanent Secretary in the Governor's Office for Development of Physical Planning and Development Matters." The job was appointed, and the official overseeing that office could probably fire the person in the role at any moment, but the fact that in the Nigerian government there were positions that had *permanent* in the title and that Uncle Segun had one demonstrated his power. Deen offered to pay my airfare to Nigeria not because I didn't have a wealthy relative, but because I did. As a working-class upstart, Deen leapt at the chance to outdo an upper-class family by hosting their American relation.

"I can't let you do that," I said. "It would be years till I could pay you back."

"It's a gift, not a loan."

Hopefulness rose within me to battle my shame-inflected honor as I kept silent, thinking. Deen was right. I was a young man now, it was my decision, and there was no part of me that didn't want to go. If I was never going to meet my grandmother, then at least I could see her country—the people and places that were the fabric of her everyday life. My father may not have been able to return home, but that was his doing, not mine.

It was suddenly within my power to be a different kind of Nigerian in America than my father had been, he who, as an immigrant, perpetually felt like a *native* in his new land. By *native*, I invoke the colonial use of the word, meaning brown, Black, other, savage. A Black American Baptist with a white mother living in an international community, I didn't have Dad's colonial baggage of growing up in Africa under British rule. Some of his depression sprang from the psychological, emotional, and spiritual strain of his experience, which he never shared with me, of being a former colonial subject who lived to see the independence of his country disintegrate in the horrors of civil war. Dad was quiet, shy, and thoughtful, but the impact of his masochistic interpretation of the American dream is the part of his life that I witnessed firsthand. The more distance that opened up between Dad and the American dream, the more distance he put between himself and his family back home, and the family with Mom and me he had made in America. Just knowing these things gave me the intellectual and emotional space I needed from my father in order to consciously blaze my own path. It was Deen's support that made this tantalizingly possible.

◆◆◆◆◆◆◆

I spoke to my father from a flip cell phone in my dorm room. "I'm going to Nigeria," I said.

"What?" His voice rippled with confusion and disbelief.

"I leave in two weeks with my friend Deen."

"Deen? Who is Deen?"

"Deen used to run IT at BPI with Mom. He's Nigerian, just like us. I've known him for years. I'm going."

"You will not!" my father commanded. "Nigeria can be dangerous. How would you know how to handle that? You've never been that far away from home."

"Nigeria is my home, my homeland. And yours!"

"Who is Deen?" my father deflected. "I am asking you again. Who is Deen?"

"The person I'm going to Lagos with." There was a long pause, a painfully long pause.

"I have to call your uncle," my father said.

"Why?"

"If you refuse to obey me and go to Nigeria, you will need family to look after you there."

"You would do that?"

"Yemi," he said. "What else can I do besides go with you myself?"

"You could meet Deen. You could come with me!" As soon as the words came out of my mouth, I regretted them. I knew better than to think my father would accompany me to Nigeria, or engage with an outsider, especially another Nigerian man with whom his shame and humiliation would be especially acute. I felt silly for wanting him by my side.

"I am here. My brother is there. I will call him."

"If you think it makes sense," I said.

"I do."

I closed my flip phone and stared at it in my hand. For once, my dad seemed to be on my side.

◆◆◆◆◆◆

My father followed in the footsteps of his older brother, Olusegun Jawando, when he earned a scholarship to study in the United States for a STEM career. Uncle Segun studied architecture and engineering at the University of Washington in Seattle, while my father studied computer science at Fort Hays State University in Kansas. Both brothers married white American women and had children. However, my father remained almost exclusively in the States for the rest of his life, while Uncle Segun leveraged his American education to build a momentous career in Nigeria.

In the 1970s, Uncle Segun led the Lagos State Civil Services as Assistant Chief Town Planning Officer. In 1981, the Nigerian government chose him to lead the New Towns Development Authority. Three years later, he became the Permanent Secretary in the Governor's Office for Development of Physical Planning and Development Matters, where he oversaw countless major projects. For half a century, Uncle Segun's work has been essential to the planning of Nigeria's most prominent urban centers, including designing Lekki Phase 1, a luxury city, logistical hub, and economic center on a peninsula south of Lagos, and later serving as chairman of the Lekki Free Trade Zone, one of the largest real estate development initiatives in Africa.

If my father had returned home to Nigeria, it would have been to many roads and city centers his brother had planned. If my father, who lived in apartments with grated windows in the low-income sections of Silver Spring, had returned home, he would have been welcomed to my uncle's compound in a gated community on exclusive Victoria Island, which Uncle helped design. Uncle Segun's success only deepened Dad's sense of failure.

Dad had told me that Uncle Segun would meet me at the airport, even though I was scheduled to visit with him on Victoria Island in the middle of my two-week trip. I had said that wasn't necessary but apparently Uncle insisted.

Uncle Segun, a small, thin man who moves slowly, deliberately, met us at a carousel in baggage claim. Fatherly, he took me by the shoulders, and we stared at each other, instantly recognizing our family resemblance in the shape of our eyes, our noses, the same features I shared with Dad. I had met Uncle Segun a few times over the years, when he traveled to the States, but it had been years since we'd seen each other and this time felt different, more complete.

For folks who have siblings, extended family is no big deal. For only children, like me, it is huge. As a father of four, parenting has taught me many things, especially about my own childhood. Part of why I felt so distant from my father is because we didn't have any family or even friends around us to naturally model communication. My kids have their inside jokes and fallouts. They comfort each other one moment and irritate each other the next. They learn from each other how to be fuller, deeper humans whether they know that's what they're doing or not. I had only alone time with my father. The monotony of it just being the two of us, for years and years, ate away at our frail relationship. But because I carried my father everywhere with me, and still do, irrespective of the low points between us, just seeing and embracing Uncle Segun at the Murtala Muhammed International Airport in Lagos was like having someone else sitting with my father and me in the Roy Rogers booth. My father might have been a world away, but finally, we weren't alone.

❖❖❖❖❖❖

"Hello! Hello! Welcome!" a man at baggage claim greeted me in a celebratory manner. I assumed this enthusiastic man was with my uncle.

"Hi." I shook the rail-thin man's hand heartily. Then I noticed Uncle Segun looking at us.

"You're not with my uncle?"

"This is Daniel," Deen introduced him. "He works for me."

"And while you're here I will work for you too," Daniel said. This man seemed more enthusiastic than subservient. He was clearly devoted to Deen.

"Oh, will you?" Uncle Segun looked askance.

"This is my friend, Deen," I said, introducing him to Uncle.

"Hello," Deen said cordially, but coolly.

But if Deen was cool, Uncle Segun was ice. "I trust you had a good trip," he said, "and that my nephew will be very comfortable for the duration of his visit in your home."

"It's my job to make sure of it!" Daniel responded, aware of, but immune to, the class dynamics at play between Uncle and Deen. Deen was the upstart; Uncle was the old guard. A member of the servant class, Daniel, I suspected, found the distinctions between men who can each hop on international flights petty.

"Thank you," I replied to Daniel.

"What the Big Man asks for, the Big Man gets," Daniel responded.

"Who is the Big Man?" I asked.

Deen modestly raised his hand, half smiling, upending the class rift with self-effacement. "You would never know because I'm neither tall nor fat, but it's me. I'm Big Man. Nigerians have a sense of humor. I'll bet your uncle would agree."

"So I've heard," said Uncle Segun, the trace of a smile approaching his lips.

◆◆◆◆◆◆◆

Perpetually restless, Deen needed the energy and movement of the street to steady his mind. The tireless activity was like a slipstream for his thoughts, a lubricant for his problem-solving. While I stayed with him, in the largest house in the nicest working-class neighborhood of Ikorodu, we got into the habit of taking long walks, mostly in the early morning before his workday kicked in.

Roadside chicken vendors trudged between cars with roughly a dozen feathered birds hanging from a string over each shoulder. Children played chess under canopies to an audience of other children crammed around the boards, watching attentively for the next move. Dried bushmeat, mostly fruit bats and forest antelope, sat on display in markets like molten sculptures. Groups of laborers, sand miners, and petrol workers carried placards protesting poor conditions. Muslim faithful carried placards too, protesting sinfulness. Everything was strange and unfamiliar and yet I hardly asked any questions—except about the dried bushmeat—because it was so strange and ugly. But everything was strange to me, and suddenly I realized how in America everything had been strange to my father. And that he was homesick. For decades, he had been homesick, and that state of deprivation and longing had solidified into depression.

Deen's entourage, consisting of Daniel, two houseboys, other staff, acquaintances, and hangers-on, all called Deen Oga, which translates to "boss" or "master" in Yoruba—Big Man, just as he had told us. As soon as Deen stepped foot outside of his compound in Ikorodu, two or three beggars would immediately descend, emboldened by Deen's repeated generosity.

"Please, please, Oga!" Men, boys, and girls in rags thrust out their hands, the lines on their palms dark as those on a paper map. "Oga! Big Man!" Deen usually gave the beggars money at least once a day.

"Don't you get tired of that?" I asked him on our way out for one of our walks.

"Yes," Deen said. "But I'm not starving, and some of them are."

It's hard to describe to someone who has not been to Nigeria, the most populous country in Africa and one of the youngest countries in the world, how alive and unwieldy each moment feels, like anything can happen at any second, because it can. Lagos in particular is an experience unto itself. With nearly fifteen million residents, it has almost twice the population of New York City. Streets were constantly jammed with cars, motorcycles, bicycles, and pedestrians all vying for primacy. The desire to go, to do—to be more than you are now, somewhere better than here, even if it's just a kilometer or two down the road, drives individuals and the society at large. Especially for a newcomer to Africa like I was, descriptions such as fast and slow don't capture the reality of a place like Lagos or Ikorodu. They are hungry places, places of hustle, of a piece with Deen himself.

Deen had numerous appointments each day that involved procuring items like vehicles, food, farming tools, medicines, and microchips for people in the towns surrounding Ikorodu. Importing those goods from the States and other countries was easy. Distributing them across Nigeria was a lot harder. Roads are bad across the country, and heavy truck traffic makes them worse in communities with the least access.

One afternoon Daniel and I accompanied Deen to the Lagos Port Complex where a shipment of his had just arrived. Deen's haul, a large tractor trailer lined with cars, was out in front of one of the port's complexes, under the protection of armed guards. Each of the cars on the trailer was filled with medicines and electronics. It was the largest parcel of goods Deen had ever moved. The items in the cars had been painstakingly assembled from around the world. Some of them had been donated, I'm sure, but Deen also collected fees to purchase items for distribution.

"Everything here will help people," Deen said. "Everything."

"How did you do this?" Daniel stood in awe. "How, Big Man? How?" Daniel wasn't kissing ass; he was curious and proud. So was I. A college kid, I understood little of how Deen handled logistics, but I understood why he did it: for his people. His generosity animated his hustle, moving urgently needed items around the world to those who were neglected, underserved.

Deen laughed, gazing at the trailer like a billionaire admiring his art collection in his penthouse living room. He never answered.

That was the first time that I wondered about the legality

of Deen's business ventures, though I never had any reason to believe they weren't aboveboard. Did he think we wouldn't understand how he had put together the massive bundle? To be honest, as a college kid then, that was a possibility. Did he think if Daniel and I didn't know anything then we wouldn't be at risk if one day authorities in either the United States or Nigeria came knocking? Or was this just who he was? Not a talker, but a doer. That's what I believe to be the case looking back today. Not involved in anything illegal himself, Deen had learned how to navigate around and through corruption in Nigeria. The habit of staying quiet may have protected him and probably allowed him to thrive, but I was also beginning to understand that what made him an effective and brilliant businessman in Nigeria may have just made him appear a bit shady in the States.

◆◆◆◆◆◆◆

Invited to the wedding of an acquaintance, Deen sent me along with part of his entourage to the reception instead. Daniel presented the bridegroom with a substantial cash gift on Deen's behalf and, as Deen had expected, our little group was treated like a royal delegation.

Geles adorned women's heads at every turn, tied in bows and worn as turbans, halos, and in large fanlike shapes. Men sported traditional filas, some of solid colors, but most of them had geometric designs that were beautiful and abstract art. The dashiki shirts, agbada traditional wear, and iborun sashes increased my sense that Nigerians wore art while I, in dress pants and a collared shirt, wore ordinary clothes.

We were served at the same time as the immediate family and offered seconds before many of the attendees had their first plate. The bride, who changed her outfit at least three times, each dress making her look more beautiful, dominated the dance floor, surrounded by her bridesmaids. I danced, flirted, and danced some more. The night was so strangely wonderful that each wedding I've attended since transports me back to this one. Unfortunately, those traces of joy are streaked with the trauma of what followed.

Just as bombers in the Middle East often choose weddings and funerals to stage horrific violence, Nigerian police often stake out weddings and other gatherings in pursuit of ransoms and bribes. On the way back to Deen's from the wedding, the police pulled us over, and four officers surrounded our car, machine guns drawn. The officer pointing his weapon directly at Daniel in the driver's seat ordered us out of the vehicle with our hands up. Daniel left the headlights on and we exited slowly, forming a line on the side of the road, at gunpoint. Two officers searched the car with flashlights. The other two trained their weapons on us. I immediately stood out as a foreigner.

"Who are you?" one of the officers barked. His eyes were bloodshot but he did not smell of alcohol, only sweat.

"Opeyemi Jawando," I answered. My name clearly meant nothing to the officer, but it meant something to Daniel and though he spoke to the officer in Yoruba, I heard him say my uncle Segun's name.

Suddenly, the officer who manned us lowered his weapon, just as another officer yelled: "Contraband!" A small leather pouch dangled in one hand, a short vial of clear liquid and a fistful of individually packaged syringes in the other. Jean, a college student from France, biracial like me, had been living in Nigeria for months. The past week, through a network of friends, he had ended up at Deen's house. "That's insulin," Jean said. "I'm diabetic."

The officer who had made the discovery circled Jean, and then touched the tip of the machine gun to his back. "You're coming with us."

"It's not contraband," Jean cried out. "It's medicine. I *need* it." The officer hurled the pouch to the ground and crushed it with a single stomp of his foot. Jean barely remained standing while his voice crumpled. "I could *die*! Without that, I could *die*!"

The officer who had destroyed the insulin swung open the police vehicle door and threw Jean into the back seat. An officer got in on each side of him, the other two got in the front, and they sped off, kidnappers in the night. I stood by the side of the road in shock, staring at the shattered vials leaking insulin onto the pavement under the harsh glare of headlights. My name, my family name, meant something to Deen and to Daniel, and to the officer who held me at gunpoint. Though I was the son of a man who could not face his family, my name now meant protection to me. The name that had weighed my father down had sheltered me. I prayed Jean would be so lucky.

When we got back to the compound, Daniel told Deen what had happened, and I had never before seen Deen so angry. His rage snapped me out of the numbing fog that had enveloped me since the kidnapping. Deen berated Daniel. Then he stampeded through the house to his office, where he got on his knees, pulled a corner of carpet from the wall, and uncovered a black safe set into the floor. Deen entered the combination, the lock released, and he pulled out seven or eight thick stacks of bills. Clearly practiced, Daniel handed him a nylon backpack and I helped Deen place the money in the bag. When Deen and Daniel left for the police station I stayed behind, my thoughts racing through a loop of uncertainties.

❖❖❖❖❖❖❖

The extrajudicial threats, the sheer lawlessness, far beyond anything most Americans experience, shook me to the core.

Would the French student go into diabetic shock at the police station? Would the police beat him into a seizure? Would the police take Deen's money *and* hurt him anyway? How many times had Deen paid a ransom? What if the police wanted something more than money? If things went south for Deen and the police took him into custody, who was going to save him?

Around three hours later, Jean, Daniel, and Deen returned. The three of them looked exhausted and sweaty, but more or less okay, even Jean. After the police station, they stopped at a doctor where they picked up a supply of insulin. When I saw that Deen's hand was bandaged, I asked him what the doctor said.

"Yes," Deen said, a strained smile at the night he had survived breaking through his weariness. "Never send others to a wedding you've been invited to. Next time, accept the invitation yourself."

◆◆◆◆◆◆◆

The three days I spent with Uncle Segun at his Victoria Island compound were a powerful antidote to the events of the night the police held us up. It was full of warm welcomes and family. Cousins, aunts, and uncles called me *Yemi, Yinka's son*, and all around me, in my uncle's palatial home with views of the Atlantic, secured behind massive gates, I witnessed evidence of the wealth that had shamed my father, and also why Dad remained emotionally poor for so long. The worst part about my father's absence was how much he was missed. Here, all that mattered was the richness of presence, of warm embraces and prostrated greetings to the elders.

Uncle's career had earned him money and status, but his decision to return to Nigeria had a lot to do with that. Deen worked in America but frequently returned home. Uncle Segun and Deen had one important thing in common despite their class differences: they were not casualties of the American dream.

Everyone remembered Dad as funny and lighthearted. He loved record stores and the sound of the great African singer Fela Kuti back in the sixties. I discovered this from Aunty Muinat, my dad's older sister who lived in Kaduna, in the northern part of Nigeria, a woman who drove more than fifteen hours to visit me. Dad's preference for tea came from how many pots he shared with his mother on the veranda of their riverbank home in Ibadan, about two hours north of Lagos, while listening to records, another uncle remembered. Uncle Segun had been surprised when my father chose a technology career. "Yinka always seemed like a professor or an artist," he said.

Uncle was right. Dad was pensive, solitary, and, frankly, a daydreamer, just as you might expect an artist to be. Uncle's comment made no excuse for my father, but it did make sense. Maybe it wasn't hustle that evaded Dad. After all, he supported himself in the States for decades. Maybe it was something I had long intuited without fully understanding. Whether it was a community of Nigerians, artistic types, or Nigerian artistic types, that was the medicine Dad badly needed. Not hustle, but community. Without community, my father lacked energy. Without community, he did not live in America so much as become stranded there. To understand my father, I needed to travel four thousand miles. It was at this distance that I finally started to feel close to him.

❖❖❖❖❖❖

On one of the last mornings I spent in Nigeria before returning to the States, Deen and I went on one of our long walks.

Beggars and vendors, people shoulder to shoulder on the street, and faces, young, old, and of every shade of brown, peered down on us through the frames of their windows. As Deen and I strolled side by side, I felt something touching my hand. I looked down and saw that Deen had linked his pinky with mine. I glanced at him quizzically without pulling my finger away.

"Ah, you don't know what that means, do you?" he said as we stood in the street, our pinkies hooked, bikes and motorcycles swerving around us.

Amused and awkward, I answered, "No idea."

"This is how Nigerian men show affection to their closest friends." Deen smiled.

Deen was the wizard in the server room. Deen was the Big Man who could move much-needed cargo around the world. Deen was the man who rescued kidnapping victims from the police. I was just a college kid who wanted to know something about our shared heritage. "Me? *I'm* one of your closest friends?"

He hooked my pinky tighter. "Yes."

By holding this tiny part of me, Deen held one of the biggest parts, the one that sought affection, connection, and family. The piece of me that hustled most of my life for those things stopped hustling for them in that moment. I had them all in Deen. Deen signaled to every Lagosian who could see us on the street that day that he also had found those things in me. At that moment, I began to understand what it meant to be a Nigerian.

6

BARACK OBAMA

I SETTLED IN ONE HOT MARYLAND EVENING AT THE TAIL END of July to watch some Democratic National Convention speeches. For a political newcomer the theatrics of the state roll calls, the correspondents interviewing both the new and seasoned political leaders from across the country, and the quirky and creative swag of the delegates became the stuff of compulsive TV-watching. But the moment I got settled on my couch, I wanted a snack, so I headed to my kitchenette and microwaved a bag of popcorn. When I returned to the living room, a man from Illinois was being introduced. A tall, slender Black man, his name was Barack Obama. I forgot about my popcorn.

He opened his speech with how unlikely his presence was at a political convention, given his unconventional background. The son of a Kenyan and a Kansan, this young state legislator spoke of his Kenyan grandfather, a servant to the British, and his American grandfather, a World War II veteran and GI Bill beneficiary. He explained that his father, who grew up herding goats, had earned a scholarship to study in a *magical place* called *America*, that his parents met as students and named him Barack because they believed that a name was not a barrier in a country as great as this one. The similarities between us dotted my arms with goosebumps: Kansan mother, African father, foreign names. The first time Barack Obama told his story on a national stage was the first time I heard anyone ever, let alone someone in the public sphere, share a story remotely like my own.

After my trip with Deen to Nigeria, I decided to announce my connection to Nigeria and assert my global Blackness by doing what Americans are famous for: asserting our identities as individuals. Fifteen years before, my mother had traded in Yemi for William in the hopes I would have an easier time at school. My sophomore year of college I formally reversed her decision, and now, because I am comfortable with my whole identity, I go by both names interchangeably. Watching the speech, I experienced a version of the role-model effect education researchers have documented with Black children in kindergarten through third grade when they have a Black teacher. When you see yourself in your teacher, you start to believe in what minutes before seemed impossible. For the first time, in a real and tangible way, I could imagine going into politics and public service because I finally saw someone whose life resembled mine who had successfully entered the arena. With the name Barack Hussein Obama! Suddenly, William Opeyemi Taofik Alabi Jawando didn't seem so odd.

At the speech's famous crescendo, "There's not a Black America and white America and Latino America and Asian America; there's the United States of America," I jumped off my couch and cheered like I had made the winning shot in a close game. Obama delivered the message I had been waiting for my entire life. Differences, like being biracial, and having families from different continents, were bridges, not gaps; differences and diversity can be sources of pride instead of something to hide; differences, instead of opening wounds and causing them to fester, can tap into springs of understanding and empathy.

Whether you were a Jewish kid from Brooklyn, a Muslim girl in Detroit, or a mixed-race kid from DC, Obama's empathy leapt out from the television screen and made you feel understood, affirmed, seen. Barack Obama's life story and speech to the nation evoked the aspirational America where many of us want to live, an America that I knew I wanted to help build.

A few things happened to me in the two years before I first heard Barack Obama speak that opened me up to listening and absorbing his message, our biographical similarities aside. The first was the trip Deen urged me to make, and financed from his own pocket, to my father's homeland, and then there were all the unexpected things that happened when I returned home. I changed my name to announce the internal shift. Another was that when I quit the Catholic University basketball team my senior year, I invested my newfound time and energy into starting an NAACP chapter on campus, which placed me at the center of a national controversy when Catholic denied the application to start the group. The last thing that primed my response to Barack Obama is something I was born with: a birthmark.

◆◆◆◆◆◆◆

I have a birthmark on the left side of my face that is lighter than the rest of my skin and shaped like an archipelago. It's been there since the very first time I looked in the mirror. Closer to my nose and mouth than my ear, it's noticeable both head-on and in profile, though it is sometimes barely visible in pictures.

An older woman in a colorful windbreaker at the bus stop on Wayne Avenue in Silver Spring once told me when I was ten or so that my birthmark reminded her of an apple peel. I think she was being kind. A little boy no more than three passed me on the street in a stroller, pointed directly at my birthmark as his mother pushed him, and said, "Feather." I've learned that a birthmark can be like a Rorschach test in the wild. It can tell you what people think of you and of themselves, and also how a culture thinks.

From the time I was in fourth grade until I started high school, I dreaded my mother picking me up from school. Before she picked me up, my peers, who were mostly Black, assumed I was Black like them. After my mother's race became known, a few kids still perceived me as Black, but a different kind of *Black* than they considered themselves. They were *all.* I was just *half.*

In the hallway, in class, and on the basketball court, after word got out about my mom, kids would taunt me with comments like, "That mark on your face is the white coming out!" or, "You can't hide the white! There it is!" Mostly, I'd ignore this sort of thing, but once I smooshed a kid in his temple and then pointed at my birthmark crazily, daring him to touch it. He backed down fast enough but I was upset with myself for losing my temper. Besides, my outburst had been useless. Whatever my response, from the rageful to the dismissive, my birthmark didn't budge. It was a fixed sign of my being biracial, an emblem of stigma.

By the time I returned to the States from my first trip to Nigeria, the Oreo narrative had lost its power over me. In a darkly funny way, I began to see just how African American I seemed, to provoke the insults that *Black* kids hurled at me. Also, encountering my Nigerian heritage in my father's homeland imbued me with a sense of global Blackness that I hadn't experienced previously. The trip taught me that rather than being manipulated by skin-deep perceptions of *Black* and *white*, I could choose how I would mark the world rather than allow the perceptions of others to leave their mark on me.

In his 2004 convention speech, when Obama said that we must "eradicate the slander that says a Black youth with a book is acting white," I felt my hand touch my birthmark. I had never heard a politician speak this way. I had never before felt like a politician was speaking directly to me. I had never heard anyone like Barack Obama speak before, period.

All American children need meaningful ties to their heritage, but Black children need it urgently. I see this at work when I look at the difference between Black children who can trace their family back before the Great Migration and those who seem cut off from their family history and the survival strategies that brought them where they are today. Knowing who and where they come from is the history our children need to make them resilient in the face of racist miseducation. My resiliency became fused with my name, and it remains the case today. I'm Yemi and I'm Will. The two names don't reference separate people, but rather they are different names for the same person.

My first stop back on Catholic's campus post-Nigeria was the registrar's office at Cardinal Hall, where student records were kept and amended. Like so many buildings across America's colleges and universities, Cardinal, now called O'Connell Hall, went up when Gilded Age robber barons donated huge sums to erect university buildings that expressly looked ancient and European.

By dictating the design of the places where Americans studied, lived, and worked, the wealthiest and most powerful men of turn-of-early-twentieth-century America set out to shape the lives and minds of middle-class Americans. The genocide of Indigenous peoples and the centuries-long enslavement and torture of kidnapped Africans were nowhere near the heart of American history. Buildings themselves, their names, and our names as individuals constitute so much of the architecture of our lives. How enslaved people had been stripped of their names and marked as property with the surname of their owner is one of history's most heinous crimes. I walked into that relic of a building that day, a crumbling symbol of an older America's obsession with Europe, on behalf of myself and my ancestors, intending to reclaim a part of myself.

Two or three folks stood at their stations behind a long counter. One of them, a middle-aged man in glasses, made eye contact and smiled courteously. I followed the queue over to him.

"How can I help today?"

"I'm changing my name," I said. "Is there a form for that?"

Almost imperceptibly, his eyes widened behind his square lenses, and he directed his attention downward to a waist-high shelf of forms. "We don't get that one a lot," he said. "I'll be right back."

I discovered that a name change can elicit superstition. In the shower that morning, I became obsessed with filling out the form with my own pen. I rode the metro and walked to the registration building with a ballpoint Bic, white barrel, black ink, pressed against my palm. A wire mesh cup of identical pens sat on the counter. While my superstition suddenly felt ridiculous, the pen's ubiquity struck me as a good omen.

"Here it is," the man said when he returned, sliding the form across the counter like a menu.

I thanked him and printed the name I had enrolled with at Catholic, William Opeyemi Jawando, above the name I chose to have printed on my diploma: Opeyemi Jawando. I completed the form with the signature of my restored name and the date, January 14, 2003. Before I had completely released the form back to the registrar, the man who had helped me started reading it over his glasses.

"Looks good," he said, ripping off the yellow carbon copy and slipping it back across the counter. I picked it up and stared at the thin paper, impressed with my achievement. People saw what they wanted when they noticed my birthmark. I saw who I was when I read the name given to me at birth. It was the name of a Nigerian, an American, a proud Black man.

◆◆◆◆◆◆◆

I headed to the gym from the registrar to inform my basketball coach Mike Lonergan, a dark-haired guy with prominent eyebrows and a sharp nose, that my name needed to change in the program book. He sat at his desk reading *The Washington Times*.

"Good morning," I greeted him.

He looked up, his face pinched. "Hey, Will. Your calendar wrong? There's no practice today."

"No, Coach, I'm straight schedule-wise. I'm actually here for something else."

"Okay, what's up?" A resigned contempt filtered through his features. He had better things to do than speak with me, like read the sports pages.

"I want to change my name in the program book."

"Change your name?" Coach Lonergan's brow furrowed, and the movement seemed to lift his comb-over. "To what?" he mocked. "The Man?"

As I was a team leader and starting guard, that might have been an apt description from the perspective of at least a few of the guys, but Coach Lonergan was clearly mocking me. Quick to disparage and slow to encourage, he was the meanest coach I'd ever played under. There are many types of coaches: motivators, screamers, contemplatives, all with their own take on how to get their teams to win. I had played for my share of screamers and hard-nosed coaches before. Indeed, my high school coach, Coach D., shouted with the best of them. But with Coach Lonergan it was different. His attacks were nasty, personal, and relentless. Though he had a good eye for talent and was proficient with the Xs and Os of basketball strategy, his mean-spirited demeanor overshadowed any other quality he had. He may have believed that a lack of kindness cut a clearer path to victory for the team. Either way, he was unanimously disliked by his players, and I think he mistook being loathed for being powerful. The dislike was so palpable it served as a unifying force on the team, just not the kind he was looking for. Before games the team captains would routinely say, "F Lonergan, let's go out there and win for ourselves."

"My name is Opeyemi Jawando and I have made it official with the registrar's office."

"What?" He leaned back in his chair, his nostrils flaring in disgust. "So what are you, a Muslim now?" he sneered, the hackles of his post-9/11 racism high, as he folded the newspaper and tossed it across the desk. I had been expecting xenophobia and derision in response to my name change. I was prepared.

"It doesn't matter what my religion is." I gritted my teeth, partially because of his racism and also because the paternal side of my family *is* Muslim. "I'm changing my name," I told him again, unzipping my backpack. I reached for my notebook, tore out a page, and pulled my Bic out of my pocket. In block letters, I printed my name on the paper, signaling foreignness for him and belonging for me. I placed it on his desk before turning to leave.

◆◆◆◆◆◆◆

Despite being nestled in Washington, DC's mostly Black Brookland neighborhood, Catholic University remains a predominantly white institution. After attending North Carolina Central, which is a Historically Black College, I found the lack of diversity at Catholic jarring. The largest visible constituencies of Black people on campus were not students, but university employees working in custodial, landscaping, and food services. In the dining hall after basketball practice, when only a few stragglers were left, I got to know an older woman named Renee, her black hairnet contrasting with her mostly gray mane, her friendly nature a measure of her gratitude for her position.

A lifelong DC resident, Renee was helping to raise her adolescent grandchildren whom she wanted to be home with in the evening. Her daughter, the children's mother, worked a night shift cleaning an office building in downtown DC, and both women feared the consequences of leaving three teenagers unsupervised at night, even if skipping homework was the worst the kids were up to. Though Renee signed up to work the breakfast and lunch shifts, and pleaded with her supervisors for that rotation, last-minute schedule changes usually put her on campus three or four nights a week. Anything beyond apologetic pleas for a better schedule would have put her ability to help support her grandkids on the line.

Not infrequently students treated the janitors abusively in the dorms, making fun of them while they cleared beer cans and pizza boxes from the halls, or disinfected bathrooms that students had sprayed with vomit when they'd had too much to drink. As I processed the realities of what amounted to a disenfranchised campus community, I grasped that how these workers were treated by some students mirrored the systemic treatment they suffered at the hands of their employer. In the ecosystem of the campus culture, the wrongdoing of the higher-ups fed the contempt of certain students for the workers on the ground. The empathy I felt for the Black staff at Catholic morphed over time into outrage at a college community that failed to treat its essential and most vulnerable employees fairly and with respect. The basketball players experienced shades of such mistreatment at the hands of Coach L., and the worst instance of harm I witnessed on the team centered on a bench player named Kyle.

Kyle had gone to the dentist for a routine procedure that triggered an epileptic seizure. The dentist interpreted the seizure as a violent outburst and called the police. When the officers arrived, they assaulted Kyle, leaving him with a black eye and bruised face. A few days later, Kyle walked into practice, all of us by that time aware of what had happened, including Coach L., who acted as if what happened to Kyle—having a medical emergency in a healthcare facility that resulted in being brutalized by the police—was funny.

"You look like shit," Coach L. shot at the traumatized teenager, as if Kyle had dragged himself to practice after a night of drinking. "Don't expect any special treatment. It's not my fault you got beat up by cops," he said to Kyle with a typical lack of empathy. It wasn't just that Coach L. refused to show concern for Kyle by asking him how he was doing, how he could help, if he needed someone to reach out to any medical or counseling staff on campus on his behalf, if he had considered filing a complaint, and if he needed assistance doing so. Coach L. demonstrated his instinct to step on someone when they were down, which was worse than not caring.

One evening a week or two later, before basketball practice, the team sat in a U-shape and watched film of our previous game, as we usually did. Coach L. had been more rude to me than usual since I changed my name, and I tried to ignore it, but this night he pushed me to the edge.

"Guys, look at Jawando." Coach paused the tape, lasering in on me with the red pointer, marking my chest with a target on the screen while ignoring my presence in the room. "Will's not as close as he needed to be to guard that guy. Will was in California and the other guy was here in DC. There's a whole continent between them. Look at all the fucking space!"

"A few inches," I spoke up, "is not a continent."

"We lost the game, Jawando, because you weren't where you needed to be. A different name doesn't mean that on the court you get to fucking prance around your own country." Coach abruptly shut off the television. "Everyone into the gym! Now!"

Moments later, the assistant coach was putting black masking tape on the gym floor, in the area where Coach had said I hadn't effectively guarded the opposition. As the assistant coach continued laying out the tape, he directed the team to sit in the bleachers, and I wondered what was going on. When Coach L. entered the gym, he strutted onto the court to one of the taped spots. "Jawando," he yelled, "get down here!"

My muscles tensed with each step, and anger ran my blood cold. I almost started to shiver with rage but clenched my fists in order to contain myself.

"Stand on the tape." Coach pointed to the carefully made black rectangle on the gym floor.

"Why?" I stood my ground about four feet away from him. The team was dead silent, the assistant coach too.

"That's where you should have been in the game. You weren't there then, so get your ass there now!" he shouted, spittle flying into my face. Then, like an animal seeking to show dominance, he bumped his chest into mine.

"You need to back up off me," I said, aware that Coach L. had taken us far from a university gym and had instead planted us on a street corner in any rough neighborhood in this country.

"Why?" He bumped my chest again, pushing me back a few steps. "What are you going to do about it?"

I clenched my teeth, shut my eyes for a quick moment, trying to breathe. Nose to nose, the smell of coffee on Coach L.'s breath mixed with his drugstore cologne made me gag. If I pushed him back, or smooshed his face away from mine like every bone in my body was telling me to do, I would be expelled. That was a fact. I thought about the kid I had hit for talking shit about my birthmark years earlier. And how I wanted to hit this man who was guilty of so much more, but couldn't, not without trashing my future. That was, after all, the precise outcome that Coach L. was looking for.

Finally, the assistant coach stepped in and pulled him away from me. As I tried to calm myself down, I realized how, over the past two years, bit by bit, Coach Lonergan had leached the joy out of basketball for me. The strain of dealing with his psychological, verbal, and now physical abuse had turned the game I loved toxic.

The following week, worried that I might not be able to hold back during the next confrontation, I walked into his office and submitted my official resignation from the team. In what can be described only as an out-of-body experience, I gathered my things from the locker room and headed to my car, where I sat and cried for nearly an hour. Since fifth grade, basketball has been the love of my life. When Coach L. killed my joy for the sport, he killed a big part of the kid in me.

A couple of days later, I wrote a letter to the athletic director and university president stating that Coach L. was not fit for his position, or any position of authority, especially over young people. I cited several examples of his abuse, including how he treated Kyle, but never heard from anyone in the administration. Still, how light I felt after submitting it has stayed with me to this day.

My life as a college basketball player may have been over, but this time I had quit the team, unlike when the coach at

North Carolina Central cut me before I knew what had happened. AmeriCorps and service generally had been a key ingredient in my recovery from my first big athletic disappointment. Now, in the wake of the official end of my basketball career, I looked outward again, but this time with more awareness of myself and a lot more spirit. The exhaustion I had experienced as a member of a toxic, dysfunctional team quickly evaporated. With more time to study, relax, and explore DC, the loss this time around came to feel more like a gain, a new beginning.

❖❖❖❖❖❖

A good friend, Zayna Sanders, who attended Howard, the mecca of Black higher education in the United States, had been urging me to come to an NAACP student chapter meeting at the legendary HBCU, just a mile and a half from Catholic. One night, at the very last minute, I decided to act on the invitation. Arriving at the Blackburn Center at Howard a few minutes late, I sprinted up three busy flights of stairs and eventually found the room. The door was open and voices carried. I took a seat, and since I clearly stood out as a newcomer, a few people came over and introduced themselves. When the meeting started, the very first agenda item opened the floor to visitors.

I told everyone my name was Yemi and explained I was a visitor from Catholic U. Folks smiled warmly, and the meeting got underway. I don't recall the substance of the meeting that night, but I do remember that the people there were kind and welcoming—of me personally, and of one another's ideas. When the meeting ended, folks milled around, socializing, and I decided to stick around, too. A young woman asked, "So what's Catholic like?"

There were a thousand answers I could have given. *Okay*, *fine*, *white*, would have been my top three. Instead, I blurted, "Awful for its Black staff." Eyebrows rose. Another woman with tendril-like hair that blended into her black sweater didn't hesitate to ask why.

That night at Howard, a speech poured out of me that had accrued one conversation at a time with folks that much of my campus community considered invisible. I ran down the scheduling issues, their heavy workloads, and their light pay. The abuse students heaped on them and the blank stares of supervisors they confronted when they reported the incidents or complained. Whatever sympathy I elicited for the workers at Catholic, I also got the feeling from the expressions of more than a few of the Howard students that they felt a little sorry for me for being enrolled at such a place.

Someone mentioned starting a union and I said what my friends had told me when I brought the idea up. People were collective bargaining alright, but on behalf of protecting their paychecks for their individual families. Retaliations and firings just weren't worth the risk of organizing in the eyes of these employees with bills to pay.

Riding the metro back to my dorm at CU, I thought about what I could do now that my soapbox was lathered up, and I started by jotting down a list of reasons why my hardworking friends on the staff were afraid even rumors of unionizing would mean firings: They had no support, or even independent oversight for that matter. There was no university department or office that put their needs as human beings ahead of the college's demands; there was no campus organization explicitly aligned with improving their work conditions. For years, I'd wondered how I could help the workers at Catholic. Suddenly, I realized I could start an NAACP chapter. An NAACP chapter that advocated for them would be an important step toward improving their working conditions and bringing together the Black student population with white allies and others around a just cause.

Nothing I had experienced at Catholic felt as comfortable to me personally or as radical politically as that first NAACP meeting at Howard. How comfortable I had been at the meeting is why I opened up about the labor issues at Catholic. Being comfortable enough to tell a room of people about an injustice is what ultimately began my political career.

The next day I stopped by the Student Life office to inquire about starting a chapter. A battered leather love seat and a coffee table covered with campus publications and pamphlets occupied the small waiting area. A maze of cubicles carved up the rest of the office. A counselor named Regina Howell happened to be working the front desk that day, which turned out to be a blessing. Regina knew her job and the college's regulations forward and backward. And I felt at ease in her presence, not just because Regina is a person of color who reminded me of my neighbor Kim's friends back in Beltsville, but because Regina's innate kindness grounded her, making her instantly relatable and trustworthy.

Moments after I explained that I wanted to start an NAACP chapter at Catholic, Regina came over to the waiting area, stapled packet in hand. The top sheet provided a checklist of the steps required to apply for campus organization status. The rest of the packet were forms I'd need to fill out.

"I wouldn't move on to the next step before you finish the previous one," Regina advised. "All of this will take some time and that's okay. It's more important to get it right than to rush. What you're doing is important," she encouraged. "Unfortunately, I'm not surprised we don't already have a chapter on campus."

Without pressing Regina, I understood her meaning. I had always sensed that Catholic—to the tips of its spires—had a deep investment in its white past. Regina's observation affirmed that, but I didn't feel as I read through the application packet that there was anything in it that was inherently racist. Rather, the forms laid out a fairly innocuous if time-consuming process.

There were instructions for writing a proposal and for a form to be completed by a faculty member who would agree to advise the group, if it were approved. A minimum of twenty students had to want to join. There were other steps, too, like securing space in designated blocks of time. I determined that the process looked doable and thanked Regina for her time.

"Draft the proposal and then ask whoever you're thinking of for your faculty advisor to have a look at it," Regina said. "That way, you will have invested some of your own work and you will have told someone about it that you respect. You'll feel accountable to them to keep going."

"Does anyone start this process without finishing?" I asked. Maybe I was biting off more than I could chew, I thought. A senior taking a full course load, I was also starting the law school application process.

"Yes," Regina answered, "all the time. It's a boulevard of broken dreams around here," she said, laughing to herself. "People want to start something, but then they don't have the purpose or reason behind it that keeps them going, so their motivation peters out and the group never even gets to the table for consideration."

"Where do you see most people fall off?"

"At the member-gathering stage. It's demoralizing when people you thought were your friends refuse to let you put their name down on a list. That stops people in their tracks because they realize the group can't be made up of just friends. It's the people they don't know well who they may have the most in common with."

"So I should go wide," I said.

Regina gave me a friendly, big sister nudge. "You got it."

❖❖❖❖❖❖❖

Since math was always my favorite subject in school, and I was fascinated by people, especially groups of people as I grew older, I chose to major in sociology at Catholic. As my interests developed, so did my commitment to my studies. I studied and read more, and my grades reflected that. However, I hadn't developed strong relationships with professors. The ones I had were either cool or nonexistent, with one exception.

There are just some people you lay eyes on and instantly like. Dean Hoge, a sociology professor whose course on power I took, fell into this category. A slender, white, Birkenstock-wearing Protestant who was an expert on the Catholic priesthood, Professor Hoge's faith had a large social-justice component informed by his perspective as a sociologist. In one of his classes, I read *Who Rules America? Power, Politics, and Social Change*, by G. William Domhoff, who argues that corporate power is bedrock to how American life is structured and a barrier against social change. That book and Professor Hoge's teaching of it changed my outlook on power overnight. Both because *Who Rules America?* was one of the most important books I read as a college student, if not *the* most important, and because Professor Hoge was my favorite professor, I took Regina's advice and decided to screw up my courage and ask him if he would consider advising the new NAACP chapter on campus.

I stopped by his office hours one afternoon when I used to be in basketball practice with a printout of my proposal. I explained that I wanted him to be the advisor of the group and Professor Hoge offered to read the proposal on the spot. "Part of why I want to start a chapter," I told him as I handed him the sheaf of papers, "is because I think the people who work in food and janitorial services need support starting a union."

"Is that in here?" he asked, rattling the printout.

"No. I thought that might be too controversial."

"Good call." He smiled in that go-get-'em way that the most empowering teachers have. Professor Hoge took roughly ten minutes to look over the document. After offering me a few grammar pointers, he praised my impulse to start a chapter of the eminent civil rights organization, and extended his hand to me. We shook, smiling. "I guess this means you'll do it," I said.

"I'd be honored, Yemi."

◆◆◆◆◆◆◆

Early in the spring semester, I submitted the application. I had already been approved to charter a new chapter by the national NAACP Youth and College Division, after I got thirty students to pay the ten-dollar membership fee and submitted the charter application. A few days later I received an email from Regina's boss, Mr. Connor, head of Student Life, saying he wanted to meet with me, Regina, and Professor Hoge in his office. We set up the meeting and gathered there later in the week.

"I'm delivering the news in person because I want you to understand why we're denying your request to start an NAACP chapter," said Mr. Connor.

"Denying the request?" I was shocked. "Why?" Of all the possible outcomes, this was the one I had never imagined.

"Your proposal didn't convincingly make the case that an NAACP chapter would meet a legitimate need here at Catholic," he said, his face strangely fixed. "The administration believes that the other two groups for Black students already on campus"—he held up one finger at a time and shook them for emphasis—"would make an NAACP chapter redundant."

"Redundant?" Professor Hoge questioned, clearly incredulous. "There's only one NAACP and there's no chapter here currently."

"But there are other organizations that serve Black students," Mr. Connor said, "and another one will only make undue competition for the ones that already exist." I could hardly believe what I was hearing. Yes, there were other groups for students of color on campus, specifically Black students, but they weren't political or social justice–minded.

"The aim of an NAACP chapter is not to compete with other groups, but to unite students, of every color," I said, "for justice." Not to mention that the NAACP was founded in part by white people and always had members of other races in its ranks. Several of the students I had recruited were white.

"The NAACP doesn't unite Catholics." Mr. Connor looked directly at Professor Hoge, a Protestant, who Mr. Connor may have assumed was Catholic. "We certainly don't believe the pro-choice position is justice for the unborn, or anybody else."

"My proposal had nothing to do with abortion," I said, my frustration over the university's response turning to anger. "We won't be talking about that."

"The NAACP does more than *talk* about abortion, they *support it*," he said, his voice rising. "On that basis alone, your application is denied."

The abortion argument blindsided me because my impetus for creating the chapter was workers' rights, not a woman's right to choose. Still, CU's emphasis on the NAACP as a pro-choice organization landed as disingenuous. The college's decision to disregard the rights of students who aligned themselves with organizations that dissented from Catholic doctrine seemed not only an overreach but an act of intellectual cowardice. The campus community would never learn from disagreements if disagreeing simply wasn't allowed. Professor Hoge stood to leave. "How do you think this would look if your decision got out?" he asked.

"Like this institution adheres to Catholic doctrine," Mr. Connor answered.

"I'd beg to differ," Professor Hoge said, walking to the door where he stopped short of leaving. I got up to go, too.

"Please wait," Regina pleaded before turning to her boss. "Aren't there other religious schools, Jesuit schools, that have NAACP chapters? Have you reached out to them, sought guidance?" Indeed, nearby Georgetown University did have a chapter and supported our efforts to start our own.

"We have all the guidance we need, Regina." Mr. Connor shot her a patronizing smile. "Thank you."

"This will not look good for the university," Professor Hoge said, getting in the last word.

◆◆◆◆◆◆◆

About a week later, a reporter from *The Washington Post* called me in my dorm room. They wanted to do a story on Catholic's rejection of the proposed NAACP chapter. I thought I'd misheard at first. *The Washington Post* was calling *me*? But then I realized what an opportunity this was. Besides, in the course of the interview, my outrage at the situation steadied me. Somehow I managed not to embarrass myself. I was clear, and given that this was my first time talking to a reporter who didn't work with my mother, I did okay. As soon as I got off the phone, though, what I had just done—given a national interview, because of my college's open rejection of an internationally known human rights organization—made me sick to my stomach. Equally overwhelmed by Catholic's position as by my role at the center of the controversy, I closed my eyes for a few seconds, prayed for guidance, and headed to the bathroom where I splashed cold water on my face. After drying it off with an industrial-grade paper towel, its roughness chafing my skin, I decided to go to Professor Hoge's office.

His door was cracked when I arrived. "Come in," he said, and he half smiled when he saw me. "I think I know why you're here."

"*The Washington Post*," I said.

"Yes, they called me too," he answered. "You're going to be in the news."

❖❖❖❖❖❖❖

I have knocked on countless doors campaigning for others or myself. And the experience of knocking on the doors of strangers has been an ongoing lesson of hopeful anticipation. In 2014, I found myself once again on a campaign sojourn. All the doors I knocked on were in Montgomery County. I often canvassed neighborhoods I was familiar with because I had grown up in the community. One afternoon, in Takoma Park, I had the pleasure of knocking on the door of my old sociology professor and NAACP advisor's home. Mrs. Hoge answered, less surprised to see me than I thought she would be. She had known I was running for office, and my return to the public eye had reminded her of something she had wanted to share with me for years.

"Dean called a friend at *The Post* when Catholic denied the NAACP chapter," she said. "That's how the media found out. Dean told them. He was really proud of how you handled everything, really proud."

Professor Hoge's words, in the Student Life office, when it

all went down, rang loud as church bells in my ears. *"How do you think this would look if your decision got out?"* Grateful to Mrs. Hoge for telling me this, I hugged her, and my respect and admiration for Professor Hoge, who died of cancer in 2008, swelled. A man of integrity, he exposed his employer to criticism, guided by his faith and his belief in what we were doing. He embodied what I believe God requires, and we often fail spectacularly at doing, which is laid out in Micah 6:8: "To act justly and to love mercy and to walk humbly with your God." A humble and gracious man, he granted me an opportunity that changed the trajectory of my life.

◆◆◆◆◆◆◆

During the spring and summer of 2004, I existed at the center of a whirlwind. *The Post* ran its story in early June, and *The New York Times* published its own story three days later. Then-president of the DC NAACP chapter, Lorraine C. Miller, a tall woman at six feet two with a flair for beautiful clothing, contacted me, offering the backing of her chapter to help organize a series of events and rallies in opposition to Catholic's decision. A skilled and dynamic leader, and also a giving mentor, Lorraine offered me an opportunity that shaped my personal and professional life for years to come. She knew I was starting law school and suggested I come work for her as a legal intern in the then–Minority Leader Nancy Pelosi's office, where Lorraine served, at that time, as Pelosi's director of intergovernmental relations. In 2007, Speaker Pelosi appointed Lorraine Clerk of the US House of Representatives, the first African American ever to hold that position.

Alongside Lorraine's office, the national NAACP office also reached out to me. The then-president of the organization, Kweisi Mfume, traveled to Catholic's campus and held a rally and a press conference with me at his side. Hundreds of people of all colors, races, and creeds attended a march protesting Catholic's decision that snaked down Michigan Avenue and through the heart of the charming Brookland community. Banners and signs that read JUSTICE DELAYED IS JUSTICE DENIED and CATHOLIC UNIVERSITY DO THE RIGHT THING were held high above the heads of the demonstrators. Under mounting public pressure to overturn their decision, Catholic agreed to a meeting between their general counsel, the NAACP's general counsel, the president of Catholic, the president of the NAACP, and me, a twenty-one-year-old who hadn't yet started law school. The meeting was tense, brief, and mostly for show. I recognized that everyone there except for me was a decision maker, yet it had been my actions that had provoked the meeting. My takeaway was that decision makers might decide, but it's activists who make things happen. Six months later, on October 12, Catholic reversed its decision and approved my application for an NAACP chapter. A few weeks later the first official chapter meeting took place and more than five hundred people, students at the university and the law school and others from the larger DC community, attended. Later that same year, during my first semester of law school, the chapter, advised by Professor Hoge, would begin advocacy for voting rights and a service workers' union on campus that remains active today.

❖❖❖❖❖❖❖

The summer of rallies, protests, speeches, and frankly, of being in the news put me in contact with a whole network of politically connected Black people, starting with Lorraine. I also connected with and was mentored by the deputy general counsel at the NAACP, Angela Ciccolo, who recruited me to serve as an NAACP law fellow the summer after my first year of law school. While there I became friends with Stefanie Brown, who with her husband, Quentin James, would go on to found Collective PAC, one of the leading Black political action committees in the nation. In July 2004, Stefanie, who had been the student government president at Howard, was moving back to Cleveland, and threw a going-away party in Adams Morgan at a hip place called the Chi-Cha Lounge.

I found a seat at an empty table. One woman, and then another, and another joined. At a lull in the conversation, I got up to use the restroom. When I returned, a beautiful woman with almond-shaped eyes had perched in my seat. "Excuse me," I said. "I was sitting there."

"He was," one of the three women I had been chatting with previously backed me up, delivering a hard stare to the almond-eyed woman.

"Sorry, I'm not moving," the newcomer said playfully. I stood there looking at this beautiful person who drew the pique of three other women and the intense focus of one man without batting an eye. "It's okay. I'll share this seat with you," she said, making room for me on the narrow cushion.

"Alright"—I sat down—"that will work." I did not know then that this total stranger, with whom I was suddenly sitting hip to hip, would become the love of my life. "I'm Yemi," I said.

"Michele."

"How do you know Stefanie?" I asked.

"We met at Alex Haley's farm."

"You mean like *Roots*, *Autobiography of Malcolm X*, Alex Haley?"

Michele laughed. "Yes, that's who I mean. Marian Wright Edelman hosts an event every year at Alex Haley's farm in Tennessee for HBCU student government presidents. I met Stefanie there and we became fast friends."

I sat with all that for a long moment. It was a lot to take in.

In under a minute, Michele had revealed that she had visited the farm of one of the twentieth-century architects of the Black American experience and had been invited to a hyper-exclusive event by one of the most important living American educators and activists. Without knowing where to go from there, except for back to school, I asked, "Where were you student government president?"

"Hampton University in Virginia."

For the rest of the night, we shared a chair and our lives. Michele had grown up in Queens, NY, the daughter of a third-generation minister mother, Denise Parker Lawrence, and a criminal defense attorney father, Mortimer Lawrence. Just hearing her parents' professions made me think of the Huxtables, which is shorthand for the perfect professional Black family. And yet, it was so much more idiosyncratic than that. My faith is at the center of my life. A newfound faith in myself gave me the confidence to pursue law school and then activism before policy and politics became my professional path. Michele's origins, as represented by Denise's practice of faith and Mortimer's practice of the law, represented some of my deepest yearnings. I wanted to measure up for Michele, not to her. A third-year law student at the University of North Carolina at Chapel Hill, the daughter and granddaughter of political royalty in Bermuda and New York, Michele had also worked in the congressional office of Democratic Representative Gregory Meeks from New York. I told her about the NAACP controversy, that I was from Silver Spring, and that I was going to attend law school in the fall. I couldn't imagine impressing her. I just told her my story.

When Stefanie said her goodbyes, the party ended, and the stragglers headed out. Michele and I were surprised to find ourselves among them. In our discovery of each other, we had completely lost track of time.

"Can I call you?" I asked.

"I don't really give out my phone number like that. How about you give me yours?" The next morning the phone rang . . .

"I like that you're awake," she said.

"You *like* something about me," I joked.

She giggled and that was all the affirmation I needed.

"I'm doing a voter registration drive at Wolf Trap in Virginia. You know it?"

"The performance venue," she answered, "of course."

"It's an NAACP event. The Temptations are going to be there," I sweetened the pot. "You wanna go?"

"How could I not be tempted by the Temptations," she said with a laugh.

The voter registration drive was a success. So was the date. Over the next few months, we fell headlong in love. The whole country was about to fall in love, too. Later that same week, Barack Hussein Obama gave his famous 2004 Democratic Convention speech. For weeks afterward with Michele, Obama was all I talked about.

"Why don't you write him a letter," she suggested.

"C'mon. We've both worked in politicians' offices. We know where most of those types of letters go. The trash."

"Maybe I can help," she said. "You write the letter and I'll give it to Congressman Meeks. It's possible Greg could pass it on."

I loved that she cared enough about me to ask a favor of an important person like Congressman Meeks. We had been dating for only a few weeks at that point, but it was my certainty that the letter would never reach Obama's hands that allowed me to write it. Otherwise, I would have been way too nervous.

In my letter, I introduced myself, remarking upon our similar backgrounds, and explaining how inspired I was by his convention speech and also by *Dreams from My Father*, which I read immediately after the convention. The writing on father loss touched me deeply because of my own father's emotional absence. Obama's mother's strength—how it had fashioned his intellect and sense of self—reinforced for me how the survival of my self-esteem, under the pressure of racism, bullying, and disappointment with my father, had been mostly my mother's doing. As a college student, Barack told his mother and grandparents to retire his nickname "Barry" and to call him Barack. He went back to his given name as a way of linking to his African identity when he felt unmoored. Yearning for a connection to Blackness and my own heritage, and for a concrete way to state this connection to the outside world, I had changed my name, too. Reading *Dreams from My Father* gave voice to an experience of race I had lived in many ways myself. For years, I felt that I was the only biracial kid with a family spread out over two continents who really fit in only on a basketball court. Barack's book put it simply: I wasn't alone. I had never been alone. I may have had a birthmark on my face, but the invisible mark of my birth, my life, was that I belonged to the global, intracultural Black diaspora.

Michele passed on the letter and in fact we never received a response. Yet, writing it was a cathartic experience, an opportunity for self-definition. Though I had not yet met Barack Obama, I honestly felt like he already knew me. Writing that letter helped me understand why I felt that way.

◆◆◆◆◆◆◆

Obama was sworn in as the junior senator from Illinois in January 2005. At the time, I worked in Leader Pelosi's office in the bowels of the US Capitol Building, and at least once a week, I started my lunch hour with a ten-minute walk from one historic figure's office (Leader Pelosi) to another's (Senator Obama) in the Senate Hart Office Building.

A petite, bubbly Black woman named Bridget Gibbs was one of the staff assistants and greeters in Senator Obama's sixth-floor office. From Chicago and a veteran of Obama's 2004 Senate campaign, Bridget accepted my résumé, politely informing me week after week that there were no available positions. But I kept dropping by and gradually started staying longer to chat about this or that with her and other office staff, sort of the way I had as a kid in my mother's office. In school, I hadn't really been friends with extremely smart, driven students like Bridget. Meeting her made me wish I had.

One afternoon when I was doing my weekly check-in with Senator Obama's office, I overheard the deputy chief of staff, Mike Strautmanis, and the office manager, Carolyn Mosley, asking each other who the young guy talking to Bridget was. A moment later, Mr. Strautmanis came out into the visitor area to greet me.

I introduced myself, explaining that I worked for Leader Pelosi and made it plain: I wanted to work for the young senator out of a deep affinity with his background and his politics. I told him I had an African father, a white mom from Kansas, and a fiancée named Michele. Thinking back on this moment, I'm impressed with my perseverance, my single-minded dedication to the goal of working for Barack. I'm also embarrassed by how green I was and how heavily I pitched my biographical similarities. Undeterred by the lack of any openings, week after week, I kept showing up at the office to drop off my résumé, out of determination that became habitual. The fact is, in the end, my steady presence coupled with my background finally did advance my résumé to the top of the pile.

"Wow, that's crazy," Mike said. "You've got to meet Barack

right now!" He pulled out his phone and dialed the senator's body man, Nick Colvin.

"Nick, where are you?" When Mike hung up his eyes smiled behind his rectangular wire frames. "Wait with me here, Will, in the hallway."

Seconds later, down the wide carpeted corridor, Senator Obama approached, just as trim and confident as I had imagined. But meeting my idol, I began to shake. Barely able to muster a smile and a hello, I somehow managed to stop my teeth from chattering. Barack listened as Mike explained our biographical similarities. I let out a few awkward chuckles, trying to seem as comfortable as I could while I was the most nervous I had ever been in my life. Barack broke into a generous laugh and extended his hand.

"I hope to see more of you," he said as we shook. Then he put up a friendly wave and disappeared down a corridor, Nick and Mike following behind him. I thought it was a long shot that I would ever see Obama again. But wait—Barack Obama hoped to see more of me?! Did I really hear him say that? I knew enough not to take the expression literally, but I replayed that meeting in my head for weeks, frame by frame, hanging on to each and every image. About a month later, I got a call from Carolyn asking me if I'd be interested in a position in the senator's office. She said that she and Mike had talked and they thought I'd be right for an opening on her front office team. Trying to hold back my excitement I said yes before she could finish asking. In law school at the time, I had to become a night student to take the job. But I would have gone sleepless to work in the senator's office. I would figure out a way to make it all fit together.

Hired as a staff assistant, I worked in the outer office, handling the mail, greeting folks, and uploading form letters in response to a host of constituent issues. The senior staff worked in the inner office, and then there was the senator's office, the inner sanctum, where the entire staff met for a monthly meeting that assembled many of the best, brightest, and most progressive individuals in policy circles anywhere in the country.

Overqualified and eager to work for the most exciting and dynamic figure in American politics, many folks on Obama's team willingly worked for much less than they would have made at any other job given their experience and expertise. Ian Solomon, a public policy and conflict-resolution expert who is now the dean of the Frank Batten School of Leadership and Public Policy at the University of Virginia, left his job as an associate dean at Yale to serve as then-Senator Obama's legislative counsel. Dr. Dora Hughes, the former deputy director of the Health, Education, Labor, and Pensions Committee under Senator Edward Kennedy, served as his health policy advisor. And then there was Pete Rouse, known as the "101st Senator" during his time as chief of staff to Senate Democratic Leader Tom Daschle, who had agreed to serve as the junior senator's chief of staff. People appreciated that Senator Obama was a potentially transformational figure, and they wanted to learn from him and help craft and implement policies that improved the lives of all Americans. A law school student serious about a career in politics, I couldn't have imagined more remarkable people to be surrounded by. Of course, this meant that I had little opportunity to do some of the more substantive work because there were people around who had been doing it professionally—and at a very high level—for decades.

My first staff meeting, I sat on a too-small couch sand-wiched between Kristen Jarvis, Karen Richardson, and Ashley Tate Gilmore, three young Black women contemporaries who would become some of my closest friends in the office. Tense because I was new, and giddy too, because after months of trying to get my foot in the door, my whole self actually managed to get a job. Sitting on a larger couch at the front of the room, Senator Obama opened the meeting with, "We have a new staff member, everyone." As all eyes migrated to me, I simultaneously felt like I wanted to hide and do a dance move. "We have Will Jawando here, who apparently is my long-lost brother."

Most of the office chuckled or smiled, while I blushed and felt an inward glow. Of course, Senator Obama's introduction says a lot more about him than it does me. He really cares about putting people at ease. One way he does this is by shining his light on someone besides himself, often followed by a joke. In this instance, I have to admit, a piece of me did take his use of "brother" seriously.

In the Democratic Convention speech that changed the trajectory of Senator Obama's public life and the history of our country, he passionately delivered the lines, "It is that fundamental belief—I am my brother's keeper, I am my sister's keeper—that makes this country work. It's what allows us to pursue our individual dreams." Sharing a common background, being linked by common interests, and having someone's back are all ideals contained within the word *brother*. The phrase *my brother's keeper* originates in the Old Testament story of Cain and Abel. Black men famously call and refer to each other as brothers, a phenomenon linked to the idea of "fictive kin," a term used to define those in our lives who become nonbiological relatives, out of respect or love or both.

Ten years later, in 2014, My Brother's Keeper (MBK) would become the name of the mentoring initiative I, along with many others, helped design, support, defend, and implement. Its focus was to close the opportunity gap boys of color face.

Implicit in the phrase is the ethical and spiritual obligation Black men have to keep, serve, and protect Black boys. Yes, Senator Obama may have been making a joke at an office meeting when he called me his "long-lost brother," but by linking his humanity to mine he did on a very small scale some of the work MBK aims to accomplish with boys and young men of color broadly. The goal of My Brother's Keeper, which now operates as part of the Obama Foundation, is to bring more Black boys and young men into the fold of American promise. What Obama did that day is bring me into the fold of his amazing team.

◆◆◆◆◆◆◆

Starting in 2004, mostly because of the NAACP controversy, I benefited from a series of extraordinary professional opportunities and life-altering events, beginning with learning the ropes of government from Lorraine Miller in Leader Pelosi's office. There I worked to help implement the Stafford Act, providing support for those on the Gulf Coast in the aftermath of Hurricane Katrina. Lorraine also encouraged me to apply for a law fellow position at the NAACP after my first year of law school and later to take a position as a member of Senator Obama's staff in 2005. By the fall of 2006, Michele had been out of law school for a year and we were newlyweds. I had proposed on a stormy night in April 2005 at my apartment in Silver Spring while Michele was visiting me from North Carolina. In what was probably not one of my best ideas, I decided I would start a mini argument with Michele about where we would go to dinner that evening before I proposed to create a swing in emotions. When she snapped back a retort I snuck up behind her, got on one knee, and said, "Would you just listen and marry me?" A little sick with a head cold, Michele turned around, unsure of what I just said. I repeated myself, this time without the "just listen." Thankfully, despite my poor judgment, she said yes.

Nearly finished with law school myself, I had to make my first serious decision about my career. Should I maintain my place in one of the most coveted spots in American politics as a very junior member of Barack Obama's staff? Or should I pursue a more policy-oriented position in another Senate office?

The senator's announcement of his presidential candidacy, in February 2007, was imminent. I knew how important Senator Obama's presidential campaign would be for the future of our country. But my interest remained in the Senate, working on public policy. In Ohio, the raspy-voiced free-trade critic Sherrod Brown had just won his Senate race, helping Democrats retake control of Congress for the first time in twelve years. If I was looking for an opportunity to learn and grow in a hands-on capacity across different areas and roles, I would have been hard-pressed to find a better place than Senator Brown's office, which, like all the newly elected senators' offices, was hiring. Coming from the House of Representatives where he had served several terms, Senator Brown was looking for staff who were familiar with the Senate and had good Democratic backgrounds. I agonized over the decision to apply. A mentor and big brother from Obama's office, Danny Sepulveda, a longtime Hill staffer himself, and one of the few Latinos at his level, who had worked for Senator John Kerry among others, gave me the permission and push I needed and encouraged me to go for it. I interviewed and within a week was offered a job as a legislative assistant in Senator Brown's office. Before I formally accepted the job, I spoke with Pete Rouse, who assured me this was a great growth opportunity and that I would always be a part of the Obama family. This helped me make the tough decision to leave Senator Obama's staff, while keeping faith that I would have the opportunity to work for him again one day.

Senator Brown's office had to be built from the ground up. At the initial stages of putting together an office, there is so much to do that everyone does everything, from ordering paper and answering phones to researching the senator's committee assignments and responding to constituent mail. Hired as an education policy advisor and judiciary legislative assistant, I had a full portfolio in addition to helping establish the office, and I loved the work, and Senator Brown, too. Like a character from a 1930s Frank Capra movie, Senator Brown held staunch prolabor, anticorporatist positions that pulled what Professor Hoge taught me about money, corporations, and power out of the classroom and placed it squarely on the floor of the US Senate.

I have a fond memory of sitting behind Senators Obama and Brown during a hearing of the Senate Committee on Health, Education, Labor, and Pensions, on which both men served as seatmates. In attendance as Sherrod's aide, I was glad to see my old boss. Ever gracious, Senator Obama craned his neck toward Senator Brown: "The work Will Jawando's doing in your office, I could see some of it today. I'm proud of him, though I have to say he learned it all in my office first," Senator Obama teased. I had never spoken directly to him about my taking the job with Senator Brown. In my limited early contact with him, Senator Obama didn't register an opinion about my decision. At the time, he had other fish to fry. He was on the precipice of announcing his presidential bid. Still, I was relieved to hear in his voice and see in his demeanor that he thought I had done the right thing.

I once heard a child psychologist say that if you really want to encourage a child, speak highly of them when they can overhear you. It's something that I will always appreciate about Barack. Very often, when he wants to give his encouragement to folks in the work realm, or congratulate them on a job well done, he does so like a thoughtful parent.

◆◆◆◆◆◆◆

A year and a half later, in the summer of 2008, I put my newfound knowledge of Ohio to use as I began working on behalf of Senator Obama's presidential campaign in that crucial state, focused mainly on turning out the Black vote and working with churches. I organized canvassers and knocked on doors. I delivered food to volunteers as they phone-banked and then I sat down with the ground troops and phone-banked, too. It was fun, tiring, and similar to a camp, only the activity wasn't basketball, band, or putting on a play. It was the deadly serious matter of electing the next president of the United States.

One day a week, I set up shop in Senator Brown's Cleveland office, where I handled constituency business and kept my nose to the ground on Senator Brown's home turf. With a mix of speaking engagements, formal visits, and casual walk-throughs at churches, barbershops, and salons, I heard from people what they needed from Senator Brown while I spread the word about Senator Obama. Though the polarizing post-9/11 "you're either with us or against us" mentality had taken hold across the country, the people I met in Ohio, of all ages, races, and creeds, emphasized the same thing. They wanted change. Candidate Obama was that change. He had a real chance.

For six months, in a setup that's aptly called "supporter housing," I lived with Marge, a writer, and John, an engineer, a lovely middle-aged couple who were die-hard Democratic party supporters in the Akron suburbs. Michele visited some weekends, staying with me in their daughter's room while she was away at college. A stray stuffed animal or two remained, and a few group pictures of high school friends were still tacked to the corkboard near the bed, which I'd collapse into at one or two in the morning, often deliriously tired from the nonstop grind that stretched from sunrise until after midnight, seven days a week. But it was worth it. I believed in Senator Obama with everything I had. Every day I met more people in Ohio that believed in him too.

In Akron on November 4, 2008, the night the American people made history by electing Barack Obama president of the United States, after attending a party for our volunteers and staff, I watched the remainder of the results with Michele and my host family back at their house. When Ohio was called and its twenty electoral votes awarded, Obama took a commanding electoral lead he would never give up on his way to winning the presidency. That I had lived and worked in Ohio for months made the victory that much sweeter.

Elated, my host couple embraced each other and then embraced Michele and me, as we were hugging, kissing, and crying ourselves. Compelled by the extraordinary poignancy of the moment, Michele and I went outside for some air.

The vigor of a new start in a renewed country charged the crisp autumn night with what Obama had campaigned on: hope. There was so much that was special about the election of Barack Obama, and that was doubly true for Black folks. The history of Black people in the United States, and the history of the country itself, had arrived at an inflection point. The ultimate glass ceiling had been shattered by the Black biracial son of an immigrant.

As Michele and I rejoiced and rhapsodized about all the

good the new administration would do, a neighbor of Marge and John's whom I had seen before pulled his garbage can out of his garage and down to the curb, making quite a racket.

"I guess racism is over," he shouted at us, filling the shadowy space between the streetlights with his vitriol. Unsettled, we went back inside to the election coverage, which again lifted us high with the emergence of the Obama family on the stage at Grant Park. But over the course of the Obama administration and through the Trump years, encounters with racist hate speech of all kinds has reminded me of that man on the curb with his trash. Not only do some Americans want racism to continue, they want it to flourish, to intensify. Militia groups and the alt-right are clearly part of this. And so was that Facebook post likening Michelle Obama to an ape. The white-lash to the Obama presidency began long before inauguration day and it continued to the darkest of days, January 6, 2021, and beyond.

❖❖❖❖❖❖❖

On every reality television show, at least one contestant says during the confessional interview, usually early in the season, "I'm not here to make friends." In the White House, where President Obama appointed me associate director of the Office of Public Engagement in 2009, thankfully, I did make friends. And though it was often a surreal experience, unlike reality TV, very little of it was scripted.

Salaries for White House staff had been slashed during the Clinton era in an effort to cut government fat, so many of the jobs paid much less than most Americans would imagine. To address this, the practice of detailing staff from federal agencies (where the pay is better) is commonplace to help support the work of the White House. A husband with a baby on the way, I was thankful for the opportunity to take advantage of this arrangement. I was hired at the Department of Education and immediately detailed to the White House Office of Public Engagement. There I worked closely with Paul Monteiro, who had served with me in Obama's Senate office and then on the presidential campaign. A brilliant administrator and advocate with a baby face, Paul coordinated the White House Mentorship Program for high school students in the DC region, which predated My Brother's Keeper. Each student was paired with a White House staffer as a mentor, and I was fortunate to have my first mentee be a bright young man, Andrew Haynesworth, who happened to attend my alma mater, St. John's. Paul also hails from Prince George's County. Both men of color, from the same area, working in the same field, we were kindred spirits and he would later become godfather to my youngest daughter, Ava. Learning the ropes of planning and executing mentorship programs alongside me, Paul became a peer mentor, collaborator, and friend.

My first months at the White House I also started to play ball with former Duke University player and President Obama's personal aide and body man, Reggie Love. The president's self-proclaimed "CEO of Stuff," he was humble, funny, and as kind as they come. At one point Reggie asked me to name the best men's basketball leagues in DC. I ran down which ones to check out and soon we were playing on the same team. I had been at the White House probably two months when Reggie asked if I wanted to join one of the games with President Obama. It was a turning point. On the court, I wasn't a staff assistant, legislative aide, or associate director of a White House office. As a player, around the president, I could finally be myself.

There was an approved list of characters who played with President Obama regularly, including Arne Duncan, his secretary of education, for whom I would later serve as an advisor;

Sam Kass, the White House chef; Joe Kennedy, a Northwestern basketball alum and White House staffer; and John Rice, a good friend and mentor who was a former Yale basketball player and the brother of Ambassador Susan Rice. I was even able to bring in my high school teammate and good friend Justin Harrison from time to time. Obama, Reggie, and I, like most of the guys, had all played basketball obsessively, from the time we were kids. In 1979, Barack won a high school championship, like I did twenty years later. Arne was a cocaptain at Harvard. A two-sport athlete, Reggie was a basketball walk-on at Duke and in 2001 won an NCAA championship. Basketball was common ground. I had started playing as a kid because I wanted to fit in. I would not have guessed that it would help me fit in socially at the White House of all places, decades later.

The first time I played President Obama it was two-on-two on the outdoor court at the White House. The teams were set, and it was the president and Reggie versus me and my fellow staffer and buddy Joe Kennedy. I'm proud to say that despite my nerves, I brought my A game. Reggie was matched up with me and I used my quickness and midrange game to give him all he could handle. The president noticed, making a point to tweak Reggie by asking if he was going to play any defense today. Reggie had to laugh.

Over the course of the next year, I'd be called in every few weeks to play. Sometimes at the White House, sometimes at army bases, or other undisclosed locations. We even played at Camp David a few times. A good defensive player, and a lefty, Obama handled the ball well, had a quick first step, and was a good spot up jumper. But acutely aware of how much younger I and some of the other players were, he drafted Arne and a few of the other older guys to play with him on Team Experience while Reggie and I constituted Team Young Guns.

Interestingly, in most of our youth-versus-experience games, experience won out. The president and his crew of older players used their knowledge of the game to set precise screens, slow the game down, and post up smaller players. After losing a few consecutive weeks in a row, I made up my mind that we young guys wouldn't lose next time.

There's a scene in the recently released movie *Soul* where the main character, a jazz musician, goes to a great beyond and is in the presence of other souls who are in what they call the "zone." This is a place where no matter your craft—music, the arts, sports—you are so in sync that you ascend to a level of harmony in a space between the physical and spiritual.

In basketball, getting in the zone is a rare and beautiful occurrence. When you're there, every shot you take feels like it's going in and you feel unstoppable. During our next matchup against Team Experience, I was in the zone. I was making every shot I took: threes, midrange, and driving layups. I was able to pass and get my teammates involved because of all the attention I was getting. At one point, Team Experience just started fouling me to slow me down. Even my defense was on another level. Without thinking about it, I blocked one of the president's jump shots, and took the ball down to the other end and scored, putting us over the top. Frustrated, the president threw the ball hard against the gym wall. A few minutes later when we walked out of the gym, he patted me on the back and said, "Good game." Then we laughed about the aches and pains that at twenty-seven, I wasn't quite feeling yet but that he assured me were just around the corner . . .

A common stereotype of masculinity goes beyond being hard to not feeling anything at all, or at least to feigning numbness. But the president actually cultivated his famous capacity for empathy not by stifling his feelings but by releasing them, whether it was frustration on the basketball court, or rage and grief at the horror of the senseless Sandy Hook school shooting. I always thought it was off that pundits likened President Obama to the hyperlogical *Star Trek* character Spock, who had emotions he struggled to show. Logic-based President Obama understood that the damage wreaked from not releasing your emotions would damage his roles as husband, father, friend, athlete, and politician.

The games I played with the president were also healing for me. My last experience as a team player at Catholic had been devastating. Coach Lonergan had stripped the game of joy. Though I still occasionally played with friends and in the DC leagues, the love I had for the game had been diminished by one man's insistence on diminishing others. Playing with Obama was the polar opposite. On and off the court, he encouraged everyone to step up and never go easy on him. In adulthood, my life as a basketball player has had three major beats: my failed recruitment at North Carolina Central, quitting the team at Catholic, and then playing with and against Barack Obama. With the recruitment, I grappled with failure. At Catholic, I confronted the challenge of walking away. In the White House, I played with my hero and achieved the victory of finding comfort in my own skin.

◆◆◆◆◆◆◆

I did a lot of work with HBCUs during my time in the White House, and in early February 2010, President Obama signed an executive order for the White House Initiative on Historically Black Colleges and Universities. The 2011 budget request allotted nearly $100 million in funds for HBCUs, focused on projects and programs, including an increase in the Pell Grant program, for which over half of all students attending HBCUs

qualify. I planned an event in celebration of the executive order, which happened at the end of February.

No matter how many basketball games I played with
Barack, briefing the president always meant a big day at work.
Twenty or thirty minutes ahead of the HBCU executive order
signing, I sat across from him at the Resolute Desk in the Oval
Office and walked him through the event, listing the names of
congress members and HBCU leaders to thank, emphasizing
for him facts he needed to get right for the event to go off
without a hitch.

"Mr. President, the acronym is H-B-C-U." There were always murmurs that Barack wasn't Black enough or really
Black at all, and these four letters were a litmus test. Folks that
got them mixed up were suspect. Folks who had them straight
were down. I didn't want anyone, especially the president, to
get it twisted that day. Long past being annoyed by this kind
of stuff, President Obama laughed this sort of thing off.

"Okay, got it," he answered in his trademark staccato manner, "H-B-C-U."

"There's something else, Mr. President. Today the Trojan
Explosion Virginia State University drumline will perform.
It'll be a White House first. A drumline has never performed
here before."

"Oh," the president said thoughtfully, and then landed on
a joke. "We like firsts around here."

In his opening comments at the event, President Obama
thanked the list of dignitaries present, nailed H-B-C-U, and
added after he introduced the Trojan Explosion, to a round of
laughter, "I've been told this is the first time there's been a
drumline in the White House."

The shout-out to me may not have been explicit, but it hit
me in a big way. As a kid who had grown up in the DC area

jamming to go-go music, which inherited some of its flair from HBCU marching bands, and who had found my way into the rest of my life by attending an NAACP meeting at Howard one night, for me, this event coalesced much of what had formed my identity: African American heritage and achievement, education, and music. Surrounded by the culture that gave me my sense of belonging in the East Room of the White House, I was no longer the single biracial kid with a family on two continents who really only fit in on a basketball court. There was another person in this room like me, the president, and we were surrounded by the larger community of our African American civic family.

❖❖❖❖❖❖❖

A few months after Michele gave birth to our first child, Alia, in October 2010, President Obama, on his way back to the Oval Office from an event, poked his head in my office on the first floor of the Eisenhower (Old) Executive Office Building, where most of the White House staff work.

"Hello, Sir." I started to stand.

"Sit," he said. "With that little baby at home, I know you need the rest."

I smiled, knowing he was the father of two young daughters himself.

"How's Michele?" he asked.

"Good, Mr. President. Thank you for asking." From the doorframe, he walked over to my desk and sat on the corner.

"A baby changes things," he said. "Your marriage, your feelings, your outlook, your life, and your wife. Be sensitive to Michele. Talk to her a lot. Ask her how she's doing."

My own father had never given me the least advice about

marriage or fatherhood. And now the president of the United States was filling that vast chasm.

"Sir, thank you."

"Alright now," President Obama said. "You'll do fine." And he left.

❖❖❖❖❖❖❖

The Obamas gave Alia a beautiful pink-and-white dress when she was born that resembled a christening gown. The president and the First Lady signed it and on the inside of the garment where there is typically a tag, there is the White House seal. It's one of our most cherished items as a family, and it's one I hope Alia will eventually pass down to her own children.

One day after an education briefing, not long after the Obamas had presented us with the gift, President Obama casually asked, "Has Alia worn the dress yet?"

"No, Sir. Not yet."

The president had another question: "When are you going to bring her by to see me?"

"When would you like her to visit, Sir?"

A few weeks later, our four-month-old daughter, Alia, met the forty-fourth president of the United States. The president stood in the middle of the Oval Office holding her against his chest for a few moments, and patting her back like the experienced hand he was, before holding her up and making funny faces while Michele and I looked on in a kind of blissful disbelief. Curious but somehow cautious, baby Alia kept a watchful eye on the president without immediately breaking into a full-blown smile. But much to her parents' relief, she did not throw up on the leader of the free world that day. The White House photographer, Pete Souza, documented the scene in what became White House Picture of the Day March 11, 2011. That joyous occasion and the image captured by Pete compressed so much of what had gone right in my life: with the love of my life I fathered a beautiful baby girl who my hero was trying his darndest to make laugh. I shared so much with the president. Now, I also shared with him the love fathers have for their daughters, and a love of fatherhood.

In June of that year, on my first Father's Day, Michele and I took baby Alia to church and were driving home when I got a call from Reggie Love.

"You want to come to the White House and play ball?"

"Sure, Reggie. When?"

"Now."

"Sure," I said.

"What was that about?" Michele asked.

"I'm going to the White House to play basketball with the president."

"You're going to spend your first Father's Day with the president?" she responded. We were both very dedicated to our jobs but this seemed extreme.

"I guess," I said. "Yes."

"Not in your church clothes," she said. Michele, who was driving, turned left.

"Where are we going?"

"To TJ Maxx to pick you up a T-shirt and shorts."

I laughed. "It's a good thing I keep my sneakers in the car."

"Yes," said Michele. "Good move."

At the store, I picked up some gym clothes and changed into them in the dressing room. Michele dropped me off at the White House while Alia slept peacefully in her car seat.

I think the First Lady and the girls had gifted the president a day with his "boys" because the whole afternoon it was just the president, Reggie, and me. We played a few games, and then we had lunch in the First Family's private residence, talking sports, the pleasantly warm June weather, and current events. It felt completely comfortable, just three dudes hanging out for a few hours.

◆◆◆◆◆◆◆

After two years of serving in the White House my detail had run out, and I moved over to the US Department of Education for a position with Secretary Arne Duncan for the remainder of the president's first term. Following my position there, I left government in 2012 to work in the private sector briefly at Discovery Communications before helping found and lead a series of organizations and programs that grew the mentoring work of My Brother's Keeper outside of the administration and across the country, including on my home turf in Montgomery County. Like the president, I had set my sights on running for office, and like the president, I experienced a bruising loss my first time on a congressional ballot. But now, nearly twenty years on from that first hallway meeting with then-Senator Obama, the takeaway that I hold close has more to do with family than politics.

"Call me Uncle Barack," the president told my girls at the White House Easter Egg Roll in April 2014, and floored by his invitation to kinship, my mind returned to that first staff meeting in his Senate office when he introduced me as his "long-lost brother." Starting in the summer of 2004, when I first read *Dreams from My Father*, I considered myself, as the saying goes, Barack Obama's "brother from another mother." It took hearing my children call the president "Uncle Barack" to realize that the mother I share with him is America.

7

OLAYINKA JAWANDO

FOR A DECADE, I HAD WRITTEN OFF ANY POTENTIAL FOR A real emotional connection with my father. I thought of the two of us as being *estranged* from each other. But in a dictionary sense, to be estranged would have meant that we had once been close. The truth is we had been strangers for as long as I could remember. Michele ached for me when I told her how empty my relationship with my father had always been, but she also hurt for Dad. "Can you imagine what he was going through to treat you and your mother that way?" she would say. The truth was that I had barely considered his side of things. I was so busy judging him, and caught up in a narrative about the many ways that he had failed me. Michele's empathy put a mirror to my own feelings of withdrawal and defensiveness.

◆◆◆◆◆◆◆

The fall and winter of 2004, Michele and I spent every weekend that we could together. Michele drove the eight-hour round trip between North Carolina and DC more regularly than I did. In her last year of law school, she had her academics in hand while I was adjusting to the 1L course load. Practicalities aside, Michele's ability to act definitively, whether it was calling me the morning after we met, or driving to DC to visit, announced her confidence in disregarding the rubbish about women needing to "play hard to get." Michele wasn't playing that game because sexist tropes weren't playing her.

Sunday mornings, when Michele had to head back to North Carolina, we woke up earlier than usual to stretch out our last few hours together. The Shakespeare line about parting being such sweet sorrow accurately describes those Sunday morning goodbyes. As seen through the lens of fifteen beautiful years of marriage, Michele clearly played a huge role in my professional life. But for Michele, I doubt I would have had the resilience and resolve to drop off my résumé at Senator Obama's office week after week for months. Those of us who risk humiliation need deep reserves of emotional support. Michele's love provided that support for me.

◆◆◆◆◆◆◆

In law school, I lived in a large apartment complex in Silver Spring called Georgian Towers with my roommate, John Luke, the only other Black man in my law school class of 232 students. John got up early, worked out, and went to the library. Sunday mornings, Michele and I often had the apartment to ourselves. One Sunday morning my phone rang, which was unusual.

"Yes?" I figured John had left his keys.

"It's Dad," my father said, his soft, accented voice floating in the air.

"Dad?"

"I'm downstairs," he said.

Michele stood opposite me on the other side of a second-hand Ikea dining room table. She was dressed, as was I. I covered up the phone.

"It's my father. He's in the lobby downstairs." This was a totally unprecedented occurrence.

"Oh," she said, "what are you waiting for? Let him in."

"This is not how I imagined you meeting my father."

"Be grateful you didn't have to plan something and have to feel all nervous up to the last minute. But he's here now so *let him in*."

I walked a few steps to the apartment door, unlocked it, and left it ajar for Dad. Michele straightened out the sofa cushions while I took some dishes off the coffee table in the living room and put them in the sink. "My father is going to love you," I said.

"Oh, I know." Michele smiled mischievously. "I'm trying to give him a good impression of you."

"Hello, Yemi." Dad appeared a few moments later in the living room, looking from me to Michele. He was surprising me, which was out of character, and it turned out he was the one who got the surprise.

"Hi, Dad. I want you to meet Michele, my girlfriend."

"Hello," Dad said, and I could tell he was thinking that maybe he should kiss her hand, when Michele opened her arms and wrapped them around him. "I'm a hugger. Nice to meet you. Would you like some coffee . . ." Michele asked, unsure what to call him. Dad insisted on the name family used:

"Yinka, please. Tea would be nice, thank you."

"Yemi," Michele said, leading Dad to the sofa in the living room where the two of them sat, "you mind putting on some water?"

"No." I padded to the kitchen, filled the kettle, and plunked it on the stove. I was amazed at how easy Michele was with my father, while I was stiff and awkward. Michele called out:

"Don't eavesdrop in there. Come sit with us."

I carried in the tea and the three of us sat and talked. Michele told my father she was from Queens but day by day her conviction about beginning her career in the DC area grew.

Dad said that with how busy she must be, and how much of her energy the drive from Silver Spring to North Carolina must sap, that she had better take care to eat right, remember a multivitamin every morning, and get enough exercise. He said that he got more exercise than he bargained for as a homeowner, sweeping his stoop, picking up litter here and there, and tending lilies he planted in front of his townhouse, not to mention the time he spent on his feet at the Walter Reed Medical Institute, where he had worked as a contractor for the last few years. This was one of the steadiest positions he had held in his three decades in America.

The early 2000s were a turning point for Dad. While I was in college, he landed his IT contractor job at Walter Reed and bought a new-construction three-bedroom townhouse in Baltimore through a first-time home ownership program. The townhouses were built at the historic Perkins Square, in West Baltimore, a stone's throw from several public housing projects near the intersection of Pennsylvania Avenue and Martin Luther King Jr. Boulevard. Dad thought little of the Chris Rock joke, "If you're on MLK Boulevard, run!" a comment that dramatizes the chasm between Dr. King's nonviolence stance and the gun violence that it is commonly believed occurs on streets named for MLK, largely in Black communities. I prefer to think about how my father, a Black immigrant from Africa, achieved his American dream of home ownership on MLK Boulevard.

Dad and Michele's easy conversation breezed us all through the morning, putting Michele past time to get on the road. After Dad and I walked her down to her car and saw her off, I said, "Dad, why did you come by? You never do this sort of thing."

He averted my question. "I really like Michele," he said. "I've also been thinking about something."

"Yes?" I said, coaxing.

"I want to visit Nigeria in January, in the New Year."

Dad's travel plans were what I'd waited my whole life to hear from him. Since I had visited Nigeria with Deen in 2002, I'd been trying to persuade Dad to go. But I never thought he would actually do it. This was the happiest I can ever remember him making me, yet I was so startled, all I could say was, "Dad, that's great. Just great."

"That's why I came over today. To ask you to travel with me. Will you come with me, Yemi?"

"Of course, Dad." I smiled. "I've been waiting for this trip for a long time."

That evening, on the phone with Michele, I knew what I wanted to do. I wanted to invite her to Nigeria. It wasn't just that she and Dad seemed to hit it off. Thinking back on the morning with the two of them, I realized that in Michele's presence, I had gotten along better with Dad. There were no awkward silences or sniping or self-pity. He showed immediate concern for Michele, that business about the vitamins was always his way, but toward her it was without judgment. I saw him behave with Michele how he almost never was with me: positive and upbeat. But what would I do if Michele said no? What would that say about her feelings for me? I dialed her and was so relieved when she answered after a few rings.

"Hey."

"I have something to ask you."

"The drive was fine."

"No, not about the drive."

"Then what?"

Silence filled the line for a couple of beats.

"Yemi? You there?"

"My father and I are going to Nigeria in January. I want you to come with us. Will you? Please."

"Yes," Michele said without hesitation. "Yes."

"I don't know who has made me happier today. You or my father," I said. I heard Michele smile through the phone, the way she does now when she's talking to our kids on her way home from work. "Long as you're happy," she said. "That's what matters."

"No, you're what matters. *Michele Matters*, listen to that," I said. "Sounds like a talk show."

"Oh, Yemi," she giggled. "I'm going to file that one away."

❖❖❖❖❖❖❖

We made the flight reservations for early January, and the night before we left, Michele and I stayed over at my father's house. We talked softly in the living room while he packed upstairs.

"He's nervous," I said. "You hear him pacing up there?"

"Ceilings creak, Yemi. Besides, he's entitled to be a little wary. He hasn't been home in nearly thirty years. This trip means something to you, but I don't know if we can really imagine what it means to him. Or what he's had to deal with to decide to go home. Or what I've had to deal with to go with you on this trip."

"Like what?" I tensed.

"Mortimer Lawrence's cross-examination."

"Your father?"

"Yes. He trusts me, but before we got there he asked me how well I knew you, if I had a preparedness plan if something went wrong in Lagos, and if I thought love could save the day."

"Well, do you?"

"Yes, to both. I do have a preparedness plan, and I do think love can save the day."

"What's your preparedness plan?"

"Love saves the day." Michele laughed, and we hugged.

If Michele hadn't been there beside me, hearing Dad go from room to room in search of things that he in all likelihood had already packed, I would have been annoyed. Instead, guided by her decency, I went upstairs to check on him. He was staring at his empty black Samsonite suitcase that he had bought for the trip, opened flat on the bed, his clothes neatly arranged but not yet packed. I stood on the threshold of his spartan bedroom, which I had never seen before. There was only a single picture tucked in the corner of an oblong dresser mirror, and it was a wallet-size one of me. In giant, brown plastic frames, I must have been in third grade.

"Dad, you okay?"

"I just don't want to forget anything," he answered. "How's Michele?"

"Michele is a brave woman. She's agreed to take an international trip with me to an unstable country after barely six months of dating."

Dad chuckled, and parted his lips like he wanted to say something, but then just looked at me, distracted. I wondered if he was thinking that *he* was the brave one for going back to Nigeria after so many years, but that he wasn't ready to make such an admission because it would have implied cowardice. But rather than risk upsetting him, I decided to let it go.

"Night, Dad," I said, as he continued to stare at the inside of his suitcase, looking for something that seemed intangible, something he may well have left back in Nigeria when he first came to Kansas to study thirty-two years earlier.

◆◆◆◆◆◆

My parents' unlikely romance began in Hays, Kansas, about two hours from Wichita. A former frontier town with about twenty thousand residents, Hays had its origins in the bloody period of Manifest Destiny. In the 1860s and '70s, the town's residents included Calamity Jane, Buffalo Bill Cody, Wild Bill Hickock, and General George Armstrong Custer. A hundred years later, in the 1970s, when my parents met, fast guns had been exchanged for fast food, and the genocidal circus characters were replaced by college students.

My mother, a Fort Hays State student, worked at a local Hardees to pay tuition in her hometown, while Dad had won a scholarship to study there. I had to visit Nigeria to have a sense of how dramatically different it was from Silver Spring, let alone 1970s Kansas, where most everyone was white, the temperature regularly dropped below zero in the winter, and something called Greek life didn't refer to ancient philosophers but to drinking parties and mischief. Beyond the fraternities on campus, hard drinking was a fact of life in places that rose up around saloons and mining sites. A Nigerian who was raised Muslim, my father probably found the overuse of alcohol unsettling, while also being drawn to what his own culture deemed forbidden. That's why I wasn't surprised to hear from my mother when I started writing this book that my parents had met in a bar frequented by immigrant students called Daisy Mae's. The forbidden fruit for my father may have been the alcohol, while for my mother, it could have been an integrated setting.

One night at Daisy Mae's, the affair ballad "Me and Mrs. Jones" by the crooner Billy Paul cleared the dance floor. Partly as a joke and partly because she found the song's lyrics about a man second-guessing the affair he's having with a married woman tragic, Mom hit the empty dance floor alone, swaying and spinning her heart out under the disco ball, her long brown hair swirling with her. Dad snapped up the chance to join Mom, a cute brunette with a heart-shaped face and beautiful skin. Mom says she liked Dad right off because he was fun-loving enough to join her on that dance floor. I think Dad liked Mom for being quirky and free-spirited enough to dance alone, for not being afraid to stand out.

Mom, open-minded and a gifted painter, majored in graphic art and saw things differently from most other people. When Dad, a handsome man from another world, appeared in her midst, she was ready to give him a chance.

There was no love for interracial couples in the American heartland when they met in 1975. Just a few years earlier, in 1967, the Supreme Court had struck down all state laws banning interracial marriage in the historic *Loving v. Virginia* case, on the grounds that they violated the Due Process and Equal Protection Clauses of the Fourteenth Amendment. So the law protected my parents' marriage, but it could not protect them from prejudice.

My maternal grandfather, an amateur boxing champion who made his living as a street sweeper, was absolutely adored by my mother. Despite their close relationship, he refused to even speak to my father. One time my father dropped Mom home after a date. Dad, very much the gentleman, got out of the car, opened the passenger-side door, and took Mom's hand to help her out of the car. My parents came up the walk to the porch where my grandfather stood silent, watching. The two men looked each other in the eye but said nothing. My mother went into the house without a word to her father. Within the family, she and her parents dealt with the situation in the most midwestern of ways: they didn't talk about it.

Not everyone in my mother's family felt as her father did. After my parents graduated from college, my aunt Mary, my mother's sister, convinced them to move to Washington, DC. She sold them on the idea of economic opportunity in the nation's capital. My aunt believed that the DC area would be more welcoming to the newlywed interracial couple than Kansas, where my parents were stared at every time they went out in public. In 1983, the year I was born, my parents settled in the Long Branch community of Silver Spring, Maryland.

Just a mile away from the more affluent downtown areas of Silver Spring, Long Branch had a reputation for welcoming newcomers, especially people of color. By the 1980s, thousands of immigrants, attracted by low-cost housing and the prospect of upward mobility, were flocking to Long Branch from all over Africa, Central America, and the Caribbean. The flipside of low rents, though, was shoddy apartments, poorly maintained. One of them, at 8500 New Hampshire Avenue, became our home. There were jobs, but not necessarily enough for everyone, and increased economic desperation produced a rise in street crime. If Hays was defined by the history of white supremacy's murderous conquest over land and people, Long Branch suffered from yet another pathology of American life: the imperative to segregate.

For decades, redlining had kept Black folks and other people of color from living in downtown Silver Spring. That notorious real estate and banking practice denied loans to non-whites trying to buy homes in an area where redlined maps contrived by banks carved out chunks of the city for whites only. My parents' marriage faltered under the weight of the racially circumscribed opportunities of Long Branch. Their shared experience deepened their understanding of racism, but those lessons didn't translate into wisdom that helped them strengthen our life as a family. Adversity can present opportunities for us to grow as human beings, but sometimes we have to do that growing apart. That's what happened to my parents.

◆◆◆◆◆◆◆

The cab ride to the airport had been silent except for the talk radio show the driver left on the dial. At the top of the hour, the news had two momentous items I still remember. The presidential election had officially been certified by the Senate in favor of George W. Bush. Nelson Mandela had broken a long-standing taboo by announcing that one of his sons had died of AIDS. Fathers, sons, the halls of power, and suffering lingered on my mind as we arrived at the airport, went through security, and boarded the flight. I slept for most of the time, as did Michele. Each time I shifted in my seat, awakened by a crook in my neck or general discomfort, I saw that Dad, in his window seat, was awake, staring out through the plexiglass the same way he had stared at his empty suitcase. Appearing far from bored, he was absorbed by his thoughts, and though he had to have slept some on the flight, I never witnessed him doing so.

Uncle Segun met us in the airport at the baggage carousel where a few years earlier he had met Deen and me. Uncle embraced Dad and the two men who were physically so similar—same height, slight build, dark brown coloring—clung to each other. I introduced Michele and Uncle embraced her. Three of us were family by blood. Dad and Uncle both embraced Michele as family in their spirits.

Michele, Dad, and I stayed with Uncle Segun in his Victoria Island compound. We had our own quarters and the days passed in a whirl of hug-filled conversations at the homes of three or four separate family members per day. For what seemed like the first time in my life, I saw my father laugh, joke, and smile, day after day, over the course of our two-week trip. Day by day, he became increasingly relaxed, increasingly himself.

Because he was the youngest of his siblings, among Uncle Segun, Aunt Muinat, and his eldest sister, Yetunde, Dad still held "kid" status. Uncle Segun stayed up nights till we returned, to make sure we were safe and to ask how our day had gone. Aunt Muinat, who had traveled down from her home in Kaduna in northern Nigeria, especially doted on Dad, pushing him to eat bowl after bowl of moi moi, a Nigerian bean pudding made from black-eyed peas, checking to see if he needed water, or more tea, or a place to rest his tired feet. Dad had wandered in the foothills of the American dream for nearly thirty years. Now he was home. And if his brother lived far more lavishly than he ever could have imagined, so be it. Uncle Segun's home was to be enjoyed, not envied. Dad may have been a grown man who had struggled for years with depression, but in Nigeria, I saw glimpses of who my father had been before his years in America, not just the man those years had made of him.

One of Uncle's bodyguards, Lanre, a tall, jovial man with a thickly veined neck dotted with chocolate-chip moles, worked as our driver during our stay. Often only a few miles stretched between our destinations, but with Lagos's traffic and poor road conditions it could turn into hours spent in the car. Michele and I half listened to Lanre give Dad gossipy updates on old acquaintances, chatted, or stared out the car window, soaking up the atmosphere of twenty-first-century Nigeria.

Jury-rigged shanties constructed with corrugated iron or wood lined much of the roadside. Newly constructed pastel-colored apartment blocks that resembled condos typical of American exurbs rose above the shanties and the market stalls, food sellers, and motorcycle taxi kiosks. An orange-brown dust layered the people's faces and clothes, the buildings and signs, all the vehicles, everything. Swaths of road had crumbled or had never been paved, were just long stretches of sand, which at times made the travel feel interminable. Mica, the sparkling mineral found in sand, floated in the air like glitter. The only thing we saw on our drives that was as ubiquitous as the dust was plastic. The sheer number of empty water and soft-drink bottles that had collected on the roadside made it seem like they had rained down from the sky.

The morning we were scheduled to visit Dad's childhood home in Ibadan, two hours north of Lagos, Lanre's mood was noticeably different. He was solemn as he prepared Dad for what he would see. Dad may have been able to step back into the past in some ways. But the house he grew up in would resist him. I will always be grateful to Lanre for not only taking care to keep my father from bodily harm, but for doing the best he could to safeguard his emotions, too.

"Yinka, the property has been rented out, many families live there now." Lanre turned to my father in the front passenger seat beside him. "It's not the well-appointed home you remember it to be."

"How long has it been . . ." Dad looked for the words. Like me, the more his emotions swelled, the more laconic he became. ". . . that way?" he said after a long pause.

"Your mother was the last one in the house," Lanre said, "and it was a big place, hard to keep. She insisted on staying, but all around the house, the city had changed. People like your parents stopped living here," Lanre continued. "People like them, like your brother. They live in compounds behind gates now. Cameras everywhere, security with guns. The house wasn't built for the world we live in now. It's a place of the old world, the colonial world. That's why it's been left behind."

The colonized Nigeria of my father's youth had a stiff formality and sense of protocol that overlaid imperial brutality with a sense of predictability, if not safety. The iron fist of the British had eventually been melted down by the fires of revolution, but in twenty-first-century Nigeria, what had arisen from the ashes of colonialism included democracy without the power in the country being beholden to it. The influence of multinational oil companies, Boko Haram's terrorism, and the rampant corruption of a group like SARS (Special Anti-Robbery Squad), which began as a governmental entity but has since devolved into a rogue extrajudicial one, had made Nigeria a dangerous place. Kidnappings were routine. A home like the one that belonged to my grandparents wasn't safe because it had too many areas of exposure, including a river that could be admired from a veranda, another point of entry. The elites and middle class needed walls, not gates. In light of safety concerns, landing pads and tarmacs were more appropriate than better roads.

About a half hour of silence passed before we arrived at the property. Lanre parked on the street in front of the house, where you could see a driveway once was but now was just a street strewn with litter. Old furniture, folding chairs, stray shoes, and broken flower pots were scattered across the property. Time and disregard had transformed the family home into a dingy multifamily dwelling, the Spanish roof tiles missing or caked with dirt. The walkway to the house featured tall weeds that had forced their way up between slabs of broken concrete.

Dad put his head down and closed his eyes, drained by how time had ravaged his origins. The flood of emotions was so strong within him that the most Dad could do to handle his grief was to let it come through. Michele reached out and touched Dad's shoulder, assuring him, "We're here with you," and her example stopped my own silent freak-out cold. I was fearful of not only my father's pain, but of his vulnerability and the indistinct boundary between it and my own. Dad nodded in response to Michele, gratitude crowding out his grief. I followed Michele's lead and touched his other shoulder. "You have your children with you, Yinka," Lanre said. "You are prepared."

We got out of the car, Dad pulled himself together, and we walked in the open front door.

A short man in loose pajama-like pants and a Western polo shirt emerged. Dad and Lanre explained in Yoruba that the house had once been his family's and was still owned in trust by the Jawandos. The man graciously stepped aside, letting us into a large entryway scattered with bric-a-brac, cardboard boxes, and empty food containers. People, kids, and clutter filled every visible inch of the house. More like dorms than apartments, different families occupied different parts of the endless rooms. Overwhelmed, Dad quietly asked if we could be taken to the backyard. Our host didn't hesitate to oblige.

I heard and smelled the water before we could actually see it. A once clear and majestic river ran behind the backyard, only industrial pollution had turned it ashen and inert. But that was not what my father had come to see. In the middle of the yard, at the highest point on the land, my grandparents' grave marker stood. But the tenants used the marker like a clothesline, plastering it with underwear, scarves, slacks, and shirts that had been laid out to dry. Outraged, I tore the drying clothes from the gray stone surface and threw them in a pile on the ground. Michele helped remove items more calmly and then stood apart from Dad and me, giving us her witness and our space. Only his parents' grave seemed visible to Dad as he moved toward the marker, leaned on it, and wept. As his knees buckled, I moved to his side, keeping him upright. He wept on my shoulder, and I did my best to cradle him. Suddenly, I was crying too, our tears mixing and releasing years of pent-up anger. I would never be able to meet my grandmother, but I could still love my father.

Anger at my father for ignoring me as a small boy started to melt away. Anger at my father for neglecting my mother started to be edged out by forgiveness. Anger at my father for his stagnation and disinterest turned to sorrow. Anger at my father for actually being around without always being present became less important than the fact that we were together now. My father grieved not just the loss of his parents, but his own absence in their lives. With me, the vicious cycle had continued. But here, in his ancestral home, the cycle with its great centrifugal force had come to a stop. Now the healing could begin. All it took was a four-thousand-mile journey together.

◆◆◆◆◆◆◆

Over the next two years, my life changed dramatically. Dad and I saw a lot more of each other. I joined Senator Obama's staff. And Michele and I got married on a rainy September day in New York City. The next major shift in Dad's life, after his Nigeria trip, occurred when I was showing pictures of my wedding around Senator Obama's office, and Carolyn, the office manager, who had become a mentor and friend, got a look at Dad.

"Who's that?" she asked, pointing to him in a photo with my groomsmen.

"My dad," I answered casually.

"Your father is *fine*."

"Well, he's *my* dad," I responded.

"Like I said, he's *fine*," she answered, and we both laughed.

A Christian divorcée, Carolyn ran Senator Obama's office with astonishing skill and attentiveness. Originally from Washington, DC, Carolyn began her career in healthcare administration, but soon moved into government. Before landing in the senator's office, she had been deputy chief of staff for

Speaker Thomas S. Foley in the US House of Representatives for ten years. Though Mike Strautmanis had introduced me to Barack Obama, it was Carolyn who taught me the ropes of the office. She showed me everything from where the printer paper and toilet paper were kept, to how the phones operated, the constituent response system, and, most importantly, the protocols, like how to deal with a constituent who demanded to see the senator immediately. The Senate is a rule-bound body, and the last thing I wanted to do was violate one of them. But I could find nothing to indicate that setting Carolyn up with Dad would be a breach of any kind.

I suggested introducing Carolyn to Dad over email and she agreed.

◆◆◆◆◆◆◆

For nearly a year after their email introduction, I steered clear of knowing anything about Dad and Carolyn's relationship. If things went south, the less I knew the better, and if they blossomed, worrying that Dad would hurt Carolyn, I didn't want to have to lecture him about being a good boyfriend. So I stayed in the dark about their relationship, until I encountered Carolyn and Dad in the glare of the spotlight.

A fundraising event, an award show, and for some the social gathering of the year, the Congressional Black Caucus Foundation dinner is a lavish, black-tie ceremony. The event is traditionally held in September at the Washington Convention Center, and, in 2007, Michele and I attended for the first time as a married couple. Outside the banquet hall, we were mingling when I spotted Carolyn and Dad, in *a tuxedo*, coming down the corridor of the convention center.

"Look at you two," Michele squealed as she and Carolyn gave each other kisses on each cheek.

"Yes, we are a couple. Once Yinka 'prepared himself' to meet, whatever that meant," Carolyn said brightly.

"Wow," I said as Dad and I shook hands. He looked great. The white of the shirt foregrounded by the lines of the jacket made him look debonair, like Idris Elba playing James Bond. Dad, I could tell, more important than looking good, radiated happiness.

"You know, Yemi, I don't think I ever thanked you for that introduction."

"Well, seeing you looking so dapper in that tuxedo is thanks enough." There was no mistaking the sea change my father had undergone. We had reconsecrated our family in Africa, and that somehow made it possible for Dad to open himself to creating family with someone else. I was proud of him. With Carolyn, Dad had chosen life over the half-life he'd submitted to for so many years.

"You have been so discreet," Michele said.

"Sometimes," Dad said, "you don't want to jinx a good thing."

"We are a good thing, aren't we, Yinka?" Carolyn said to Dad. Smiling, Dad kissed her softly on the cheek.

◆◆◆◆◆◆◆

Dad would come over to our apartment in the Michigan Park neighborhood of DC on Sunday afternoons to watch football, or make himself a cup of tea and sit and chat with Michele. One Sunday, Michele asked Dad very gently when he and Carolyn were going to get married. But he dodged the question. The following Sunday, I couldn't resist asking how things were going with Carolyn, and he curtly answered, "Fine," but the edge in his voice was unmistakable.

"You know that's the first thing Carolyn thought when she saw a picture of you. She said you were 'fine.'"

"I'm not sure how true that is now," Dad answered, resignation mixed with stubbornness in his voice.

"What's going on?" I asked.

"Yemi, I don't want to get married again," he said. "I'm settled in my ways, I don't need them disturbed."

"Disturbed? Marriage isn't a disturbance, Dad, it's a commitment."

"And I'm committed to my ways."

"What ways?"

"Those of a bachelor."

"You're willing to give up Carolyn because you're in love with being a bachelor?" I understood all too well what was going on. Carolyn, who remains a dear friend to this day, had told him she was going to leave him unless he committed to their relationship. He was calling her bluff, which was no bluff at all, and tragically, he was going to lose her. I had thought my father had finally broken his cycle of withdrawal and isolation. Sadly, I was wrong.

"Do you want to break up with Carolyn?"

"No."

"Then why are you doing this?"

Dad stood, went to the brass coat-tree near the front door, grabbed his jacket, and said, "I don't know how to do anything else."

"But Dad," I said. "It's not too late to learn."

"I am sorry to disappoint you," he said, before turning to leave.

◆◆◆◆◆◆

"It's not just the breakup with Carolyn you're angry about," Michele said one night over Chinese takeout, standing at the island in our kitchen. "You're livid with him for your whole childhood. You're mad at him for being who he is. Stop beating yourself up for not being able to change him. You'll never have peace otherwise. Accept him for who he is," she urged.

"How can I do that? He's his own worst enemy. His whole approach to life is unacceptable."

Michele shook her head. "Stop judging him. Otherwise you'll always be angry and that's unacceptable to me."

Figuring out how to be a better son became part of what I had to do to be a good husband.

"I'll try," I said, as I put the leftover General Tso's chicken into the fridge.

◆◆◆◆◆◆◆

I was working in the White House when I received a voice mail from Dad about a doctor's visit. All I remember him saying is that he had an appointment. He didn't say what kind or why, only that he wanted me to come with him. I didn't get back to him right away, assuming that if it was serious, Dad would have called again or left a more detailed message. Looking back, I see that I had engaged in the wishful thinking of a busy man. When I finally reached him a couple of days later, I asked him what kind of appointment it was.

"It's my prostate," he said, Dad's quiet voice made even softer by his own discomfort. He said he didn't want to worry me, which worried me a lot.

"Go on," I prompted.

"I have prostate cancer. They did a biopsy and a bone scan and they believe it's localized. That's what the doctor wants to talk to me about. An operation."

I was sitting on the edge of my bed, and felt like I'd stood too quickly because I was dizzy, but I hadn't moved an inch. "Okay, Dad," I said, "it's operable." I spoke as much to myself as to him. "You'll be fine."

"Is there a day it's easier for you to come with me?"

"Dad, make the appointment for the earliest available slot. I'll figure it out at work. Let's just get the first possible appointment, okay?"

"Yemi," his voice frayed.

"I'm sorry, Dad. I just don't want you to wait," and then it occurred to me that he probably hadn't gone to the doctor when his symptoms first developed, that he had been doing just that: waiting. How bad had things gotten for him to get checked in the first place?

"How long have you known something was wrong, Dad?"

"I'll make the appointment tomorrow and let you know the date," he responded without answering my question.

"How long has something been wrong?" I repeated.

"Months," he answered. "Maybe a year."

My mouth dropped open. "A year?"

"I'll call you tomorrow with the information." He hung up.

About a week later, Dad and I both shifted in a pair of hard gray chairs across a large desk from a middle-aged white man with salt-and-pepper hair. His name was Dr. Esse and he had good news.

"Mr. Jawando," Dr. Esse began, "because the cancer is localized in your prostate we can remove it using a technique called robotic prostatectomy. It's a minimally invasive procedure performed with a surgical system called da Vinci because of how artful and exact it is. In the old days, a surgeon would have cut your abdomen from your navel down to your pubic bone." He put his index finger at where approximately his belly button was beneath his white collared shirt and ran it downward. The gesture alone gave me the shivers, the sensation of a cold blade against my skin. "With this procedure, we can remove the prostate through keyhole incisions. You lose less blood, have less pain, recover quicker, don't have to hang around the hospital long, and most likely come out cancer-free."

"Will a robot perform the surgery?" I asked, overjoyed to hear about this da Vinci procedure.

"No, I perform the surgery, but behind a console where using the machine as my hands I can be much more precise than I could ever dream of being with these"—he held up his palms to us—"or these," he said, pointing to his eyes. "We also use what's called a three-dimensional endoscope that allows me to see all the tissues and blood vessels around the prostate and to do our best to leave those structures intact. And Mr. Jawando"—Dr. Esse looked directly at Dad—"this surgery involves keyhole incisions," he repeated. "The less a patient is cut, the better the outcomes. At fifty-nine and otherwise healthy, you're a great candidate for this procedure especially because the cancer is seemingly all in one place. We can get it."

Dad asked, "What are the risks?"

"Like with any prostate procedure, the risks are straightforward. Potential for some incontinence and impotence."

"Permanently?" Dad questioned.

"It's a possibility," Dr. Esse responded, "but it's about getting cancer-free. Cancer spreads, Mr. Jawando. You're eligible for this surgery now. If you wait and your cancer spreads out of the prostate, you will no longer be a da Vinci candidate."

"What's the guarantee that it will spread?" Dad's question made me dizzy again, like that night sitting on the edge of my bed when he initially delivered the news.

"With cancer, there are no guarantees, Mr. Jawando."

"Incontinence and impotence are the surgery's risks," Dad said to himself.

"Yes," the doctor affirmed.

Dad stood and extended his hand to Dr. Esse, who also rose from his high-backed leather chair. The men shook hands. "I need to think about it," Dad said.

"Let the office know when you've decided." Dr. Esse extended his hand to me. "It was nice to meet you."

"Likewise." I followed Dad through a suite of offices and waiting rooms to the elevator bank. My hand trembled as we got into the empty elevator and I pressed the button for the lobby.

"Dad, what is there to think about? Get the surgery."

"I think I can treat it, without those side effects."

"What? It's cancer, Dad. How can you treat it more effectively than a robot machine called da Vinci?"

"Doesn't that all sound far-fetched to you?" My father spoke with the skepticism of a religious zealot. It was the first time I ever detected anything in him resembling faith.

"No, it sounds like technology." I tried to shut the insanity down. The elevator door opened and others entered, jockeying for position. All the way down to the lobby I seethed.

My father was a contrarian and a skeptic. He didn't believe Barack Obama could become president until a week before the election and I'm not even sure he voted for him the first time around. Now, he didn't believe a machine could save his life. His three-year relationship with Carolyn had fallen apart because he couldn't change his ways or learn new ones. Now, doing things his way, I feared, was going to kill him.

"Dad, there are two things that can happen. You have the surgery and Dr. Esse gets all the cancer. Or you don't have the surgery and it spreads. It's really up to you."

My father was oddly upbeat, like he possessed a real solution when in reality, he was merely blinded by the desire to protect his manhood. This was why he hadn't gone back to Nigeria until he had a home and a full-time job. He couldn't make it work with Carolyn because for him being a bachelor had become synonymous with his manhood. And he couldn't say yes to the surgery because it might destroy the ultimate symbol of his manhood. I went from perplexed to enraged to awash in sorrow. For the better part of my life, I considered how my father's cycles of depression and isolation had affected me. Now, seeing how they undermined his life down to the cellular level, I began to cry.

"I'm going to treat it holistically with diet and exercise and vitamins. You watch, Yemi. I'm going to beat this. I am going to be fine."

That night in bed, my back against the headboard, I stared off into space, rigid with disbelief. Michele burped Alia over her shoulder. "I can't believe he's not going to get the surgery," I said over and over. "I can't believe he's been this stupid."

"It's not for you to believe. It's for you to accept," Michele said.

"I would get the surgery like that," I said, snapping my fingers.

"Yes, but you are not your father. Accept that this is his decision, not yours."

"How?" I begged her. "How can I do that?"

"All your life you've been fighting his imperfections," she said frustratedly. "You're a father now. We need to be looking toward the future of our family. Your father is a grown man. So are you. Act like one and treat him like an adult."

More than her words, her harshness gave me pause. Frustrated with my father, and also after a long day at work, which meant a day away from the baby, Michele was exhausted and now, despite the situation, had lost her patience with me. "I'm taking Alia to the nursery," she said, feeling, I think, that we both needed some space.

She was right.

◆ ◆ ◆ ◆ ◆ ◆ ◆

My father juiced, concocted vitality shakes, slurped down oils, and studied the mineral intake of vitamins. I could bring myself to ask him about none of it and he shared little with me, until he had to ask for my help about a year after he chose not to have the surgery. As the doctor warned, the cancer had spread to his lymph nodes and removing the prostate was no longer a viable option. Work missed for two or three doctor's appointments per week resulted in his firing from Walter Reed. Behind on his mortgage payments, he was headed toward foreclosure. He needed money, help selling his house, and somewhere to live. Michele and I agreed that there was only one solution: he would move in with us.

For the months it took to settle his affairs, I'd go to his house after work, a few nights a week. Weaker but still managing, Dad remained mobile, and he had a decent appetite. We riffled through stacks of bills, most old and a few recent. I asked how much money came in every month and how much went out. I sat beside him on the same black leather sofa where years earlier I sat with Michele, listening to the ceiling creak with his footsteps as he paced, the night before the three of us traveled to Nigeria. Now, we were on a different journey. He wasn't returning home. We were figuring out his exit.

"I have a bank statement, Yemi. That's what shows how much money goes in and comes out. But there's good news. I got another job," he pivoted.

"Where?"

"At Home Depot."

"Home Depot? What about your doctor's appointments? Your energy?"

"I'll make do."

He did make do, for a while. We sold his house, he set up his living quarters in my basement, where he could have privacy, and he had his job at Home Depot until he was let go a year or so later, the time on his feet too taxing, his doctor's appointments making it harder and harder to get to work at all. Yet in 2014, when Dad moved in, though frail, he still had energy, and he helped with the girls, dropping off and picking them up from daycare, diapering both Addison, who was one, and Ava, who was just an infant, preparing dinner for them many nights and putting them to bed when Michele and I worked late. Alia, who was three at the time, remembers him well and thinking back on this period it's amazing that our family got by with just Dad assisting us. Michele was working on Capitol Hill at the time. Meanwhile, I was running for the Maryland House of Delegates, and I see now that it may have been because Dad participated in raising my girls, experiencing himself the demands of having a family, that he was as skeptical of my political career and all the time I devoted to it as he was of the da Vinci surgical procedure.

"Why are you running?" he would ask. "You could have a steady job."

There were times I'd answer him like a policy wonk, going on about equal pay for women, affordable childcare, gun reform, and disparities in education. But most of the time, I kept it simple and said, "I want to help people." On hearing this, Dad would predictably guffaw.

"Then you should check on how I'm doing more often."

"Dad," I'd say, letting my exasperation show. "I have a demanding job, a wife, and three children under five. I have to check on them too."

"Yes, I know." Dad would cut his eyes at me. "I understand you need to take care of my grandchildren. What I don't understand is why you're running for office."

One night, having gotten home late from a campaign event, I went down to the basement to check on him before I looked in on the girls. Tired and resentful about his lack of support for my political ambitions, I suddenly thought of Deen. "I want to help people because I have the energy," I said. Instantly, I felt awful, aware that more and more energy was being leached from my father's body with every passing day.

"You may have energy," he shot back, "but are you mindful of how to use it?"

"I'm trying to be, Dad, that's why I'm running for office," I said, rubbing my eyes in exhaustion.

"Go to bed, Yemi," he barked at me like he was the father who had been working all day and I was the kid who refused to go to bed.

"Alright, Dad," I said, my sadness filtering into my exhaustion. "Good night."

"Let's hope on primary day you have a good night." Dad obviously felt bad too, so he tried to encourage me without apologizing.

A month or so later, on June 24, 2014, I had a night of exhilarating ups and discouraging downs. I lost the primary race for the House of Delegates by less than 1 percent.

❖❖❖❖❖❖

Another night, nearly two years after he moved in with us, Dad's legs collapsed out from under him in the bathroom. The cancer, ravenous, insatiable, had devoured his prostate and then his lymph nodes before it spread to his spine and shredded his nervous system. When I discovered him, he was lying in the hallway, half-naked, crying. It was the second time I saw my father cry, and the first time I saw him respond to feeling helpless with any emotion other than rage. I gently lifted him up and dressed him, as we both wept.

Within a matter of weeks my father lost all use of his legs, becoming paralyzed from the waist down. Unprepared for this dramatic loss of mobility, we made the difficult decision to try in-home hospice care. I would turn him every couple of hours to avoid bed sores. Otherwise, he was ministered to by wonderful, caring nurses' aides and nurse practitioners. Though for months I tried to shield Michele from changing my father and tending him at night, she sometimes did it too, and I felt guilty for burdening her with a grown man's wasting when she had a full-time job, three children, and our youngest still wore a diaper. So, every night I set alarms on my phone, on the lowest possible volume so they wouldn't wake Michele, who was doing the lion's share of raising our daughters and the emotional work of helping keep me together.

When the faint chimes sounded, I climbed out of bed and made my way to the living room, where Dad's hospital bed now sat in front of the television. Having him on the first floor made sense now. But it ate at his pride, being the helpless center of attention.

I switched on the lamp in the far corner of the room. "Dad, I have to turn you," I said, taking a detour to the cabinet where we kept his diapers, wipes, and medical supplies.

"Pillow man," he said. "I need my pillows adjusted."

To make him comfortable, we used pillows to elevate his feet and support his back. According to him, I was the best at positioning the pillows, and this led to him calling me by a name other than Yemi for the first time in my life. It's funny that we came to identify an experience that was so trying for both of us with something you can lay your head on, and hold, something soft. My father finally seemed to recognize the tenderness in me and valued it in a way he couldn't when I was a boy.

"I know, Dad, but first we have to get you changed."

He mumbled something under his breath. I knew that, in his mind, suffering the indignity of having others change him was worse than suffering with his disease. As I pulled open the Velcro closures of his soiled diaper, he started to speak.

"I know I wasn't a good father," he said. He had never said those words, or anything remotely like them, before. I think they must have been weighing on him, slowly forming in his head, since the day he came to live with us. The words had been festering like the gaping wound at the base of his spine that would soon make at-home hospice untenable. Seeing me be a present father to my girls, a loving husband to my wife, seeing me care for him the way a parent tends to a sick child— must have weighed heavily on him.

Then he turned to look at me. "I'm sorry," he said. There was certainty in his voice, but his eyes looked for reassurance.

I readjusted his pillows. "Now, Dad, I wouldn't be here changing your diaper at two in the morning if I didn't love you," I said, trying to both assure him that I did love him and lighten the mood with a joke. We both let out a chuckle as we began to cry. The physical strain and emotional stress of caring for my father had broken my love for him down into its most essential part, the pure acceptance that Michele had so wanted me to find. I could not change or save him. I could only love him, and finally, in the end, I surrendered to that.

◆◆◆◆◆◆◆

Watching someone you love die is like watching a rising tide slowly pull them into a vast ocean. Every wave that comes in slowly carries them farther away from you, and you never know which one will take them away for good. After about six weeks of in-home hospice, the around-the-clock care became too much and we had to move Dad to a hospice facility. By the end, Dad could barely open his eyes or sit up. The girls would offer him sips of water from a small piece of sponge, but his body was shutting down, and the sips he took were just to see the joy on their faces.

On April 29, 2017, the nurses helped us move my father's bed outside so that he could enjoy a beautiful spring afternoon. As the girls played on the hospice facility's grassy back lawn, I asked my father for permission to leave earlier than I normally would have because I had agreed to give a speech at a meeting of Nigerian lawyers. My father blinked his understanding. I kissed him on the forehead and told him Pillow Man would be back tomorrow.

At two o'clock in the morning, my phone rang. A nurse said that my father had passed. I had known the call would come at any time, every day for weeks, but I still wasn't prepared for it when it actually arrived. Stunned by the news, I got dressed and woke Michele. She wanted to come with me, and I needed her at my side, so we called a nearby member of our church family to see if she could stay with the girls. Like an angel, she appeared at our doorstep within minutes.

In the hospice, I went to my father's lifeless body and touched his hand. Olayinka Ishola Jawando was there yet gone, but this was no longer the absent presence that he was in my childhood. The man lying lifeless on the bed didn't make me fold up my feelings till they were so small they could not be found. I stood there and I hurt. Once the first wave of pain subsided, I felt calm, even relieved, because his suffering was over. And our struggle was over, too. I had done everything I could for him and he had accepted my care. At the end, we bore witness to our long, fraught relationship with love and integrity.

◆◆◆◆◆◆◆

In 2018, against more than thirty other Democrats, I won the race for an at-large seat on the Montgomery County Council. A week later, at the council office building for orientation, I met two security guards who worked there, both of whom were West African immigrants. I stopped to chat with them, one man from Nigeria and another from Cameroon.

"This is a Nigerian name," the Cameroonian said as he read my ID to sign me into the building.

The other guard quickly added: "I'm Nigerian."

Simultaneously sheepish and full of pride, I said, "I'm second generation. And I just won a council race. That's why I'm here."

Both men congratulated me heartily and their presence felt auspicious, like the ancestors sent me greeters from the diaspora.

"What will you wear to your inauguration?" the Cameroonian asked. The Nigerian, with perfect conviction, answered for me:

"You will wear traditional clothing." The man's accented voice, quiet and strong, reminded me of Dad's, and for the briefest of moments I felt my father's presence. In 2016, Dad saw me lose my second race for Maryland's Eighth Congressional District. He wasn't alive to see me win this one, but when I was inaugurated as a Montgomery County councilmember I decided right then and there he would be with me because I would make my Nigerian heritage visible. I would wear traditional Yoruba clothes. I would wear an agbada to honor both the larger immigrant community of Montgomery County and my father.

On December 3, 2018, I was sworn in as a Montgomery County councilmember, and on the podium, seated beside my colleagues, I thought of how much I missed Dad and how much I wanted him to see what I had accomplished, not in spite of him but because of him. Elected to serve the more than one million people in the community where my parents had come to escape prejudice and racism but also endured it, where I had grown up grappling with those same things, and where I now had a mandate as a public servant to address systemic racism head-on, I can never know what it would have meant to Dad, what he would have said, to see me not only win, but wear the traditional dress of his homeland when I crossed the finish line. But I have an opportunity to write here what I wanted to tell him, so I will.

Connecting to you has been some of the most important work of my life. Rebuilding our relationship was made possible by you, Dad, and by my six other Black fathers who helped lead me back to you.

At the end, you understood your importance to me. One thing I wish I had an opportunity to share with you while you lived was how essential Joseph Jacob, Mr. Williams, Jay Fletcher, Wayne Holmes, Deen Sanwoola, and Barack Obama have been in my life, how much of their energies and spirits and love each of these very different men has gallantly given me, your son. Each of these men, including you, Dad, profoundly impacted my sense of self, and when I say self I mean my Black fathers individually imparted to me a certain kind of knowledge about the self, that far beyond being a survival skill, constitutes a tool kit designed expressly so I could thrive.

Joseph restored my self-esteem after you left by

providing me with a sense of identity. Mr. Williams showed me what self-respect looks like after I began to doubt, because of the racism I experienced, whether I was deserving of respect at all. Jay taught me that self-expression is preferable to stuffing your feelings down. Wayne helped me tap into the self-discipline of faith. Deen showed me how far beyond a single individual self-motivation can reach. For me, our nation, and the whole world, Barack Obama is a shining example of self-realization. And to you, Dad, Olayinka Jawando, you taught me that self-examination is the key to a fulfilling, rich life.

The benefit of having more than one parent—and if you're me, seven fathers—is that so much of how you see and experience the world is an expression of how their influences have played off one another. There's no doubting the African proverb "It takes a village to raise a child." My experience bears out that the members of a child's village don't necessarily need to know one another well or at all to effectively get the job done. How a village of acquaintances and strangers alike can raise a child is through acts, big and small, of kindness and mentorship.

◆◆◆◆◆◆◆

To My Seven Black Fathers, I say thank you.

ACKNOWLEDGMENTS

I first want to thank God for the strength, insight, and healing I needed to write this book.

To my wife, Michele, the rock of our family, without whom none of this would have been possible: From reading chapters in between work, life, and children's bedtimes, to sending me critiques and encouragements, this book doesn't happen without you. I love you. To our children, Alia, Addison, Ava, and William Isaiah, I love you more than the heart should allow. I pray this book helps you to understand your father and your heritage. To my parents, Kathy and Joseph Jacob, and my parents-in-love, Mort and Denise Lawrence, thank you for your constant support and unfailing love.

To my Jawando, Saheed, and Animashaun family across the world, especially Auntie Debo and Omolola, thank you for helping me appreciate and value our deep roots. To my Gross and Polifka family, thank you for loving and grounding me. There are some family you're born with and others you acquire along the way, and I've been blessed with many on my journey, including my sisters, Erin, Maya, and Lisa, and my brothers, Neil, Mac, Luke, Steve, Mike, Andrei, and Eli.

I've also been blessed with a strong group of peer mentors and friends who have helped hold me accountable and supported me in good times and bad. Thank you, Paul Monteiro, Virgil Miller, David Johns, and Aaron Jenkins; we've come a long way from the early days of organizing the first meetings of African American Men on the Hill. Justin Harrison, Kwasi

Asare, John Luke, David Duckenfield, and Chris Langhorne, thank you for always being there and for the birthday golf trips. My sisters Tishaura Jones, Stacey Abrams, Shawna Watley, Tami Buckner, Karen Richardson, Brooke Langhorne, and Danielle Booker, thank you for picking up when I call and putting up with my foolishness!

My West African crew, Ayo Tometi, Bozoma Saint John, Luvvie Ajayi Jones, Tiffany Aliche, Jessica Matthews, Pops Mensah-Bonsu, Stanley Lumax, Teju (TJ) Adeshola, Justina Omokhua, Jubril Agoro, Abiola Oke, Tonjé Bakang, Funa Maduka, Cynthia Erivo, and Yvonne Orji: You continue to inspire me with your excellence and have been there for me in the moments when I needed it most.

To the ice-cold brothers of Alpha Phi Alpha Fraternity, especially my line brothers Talib, John, James, Carlos, and Michangelo, your examples of servanthood and mentorship guide me toward the light always.

In writing and in life sometimes you just get stuck. And then you have friends like Ibram Kendi and Jelani Cobb who help you move forward from that place. Thank you for the ways your brotherhood showed up as I wrote this book.

While I tell my story through the lens of my seven Black fathers, I've been blessed with many mentors, including Veryl Miles and Regina Jefferson. The late congressmen Elijah Cummings and John Lewis stepped up and supported me and in doing so literally changed my destiny. Similarly, our dearly departed friends and mentors Cassandra Butts and Gwen Ifill saw something in me that I still strive to be worthy of.

Senator Sherrod Brown, Speaker Nancy Pelosi, Congressman Greg Meeks, Congressman James Clyburn, Secretary Arne Duncan, Ambassador Ertharin Cousin, Joyce Brayboy, Jay Heimbach, Lorraine Miller, Paul Braithwaite, Michael Strautmanis, Danny Sepulveda, Ian Solomon, Steve Robinson, Jim

Shelton, Tony Miller, John Wilson, Bishop Darlingston Johnson, and Darren Briscoe, your mentorship has shaped who I am.

To all those I've been privileged to mentor, especially Marvin Figueroa and Andrew Haynesworth, thank you for giving me as much as or more than I gave you. Ian and Anthony, I will never forget you and will remember that the work of mentorship does not end.

I've also been fortunate to work with a great group of team members in my various political and elected roles, including my first campaign manager, Jon Randall, who passed away unexpectedly in 2019. Jon took my belief in what was possible and put a plan around it. Thank you, Khalil Thompson, Aubrey Sylvester, and Cecily Thorne, for your support and leadership of so many #TeamJawando staff and volunteers who have helped execute my vision for a more equitable and inclusive community.

To the village that helped me bring this book to fruition: My editor, Ileene Smith, who believed in my story years before I could articulate it for myself. Your keen eye, deep insights, and encouragement throughout this process were invaluable. Tanya McKinnon, my agent, soul sister, and enduring source of advice, confidence, and love, I would have never assembled this story and been able to tell it without you. My primary assistant and researcher, Victoria Bond, was a wonderful sounding board and an empathetic friend as I pulled together the pieces of my life, and I'm indebted to you for your close reading, editorial acumen, and support throughout the writing process. To the FSG team, especially the publisher, Mitzi Angel, and my publicist, Sarita Varma, thank you for believing in this book and helping me share it with the world.

And finally, to my father, Olayinka Jawando. I will forever see you in the places big and small in my life. I like to imagine you and Ìyá àgbà (Grandmother) watching over us. And I am thankful you are there.